THE JEWELS
—— OF ——
THE DUCHESS OF WINDSOR

THE JEWELS

OF THE DUCHESS OF WINDSOR

———

by
John Culme
and
Nicholas Rayner

———

THE VENDOME PRESS
IN ASSOCIATION WITH SOTHEBY'S

Designed by Arbook International, Paris
Edited by Alexis Gregory
Picture research by Philippe Garner
Project coordinator: Marcus Linnell
Research: David Bennett

Copyright ©1987 Sotheby's
First published in Great Britain by Thames and Hudson
First published in the United States of America by The Vendome Press
515 Madison Avenue, New York, N.Y. 10022

Distributed in the United States of America by
Rizzoli International Publications
597 Fifth Avenue, New York, N.Y. 10017

Distributed in Canada by Methuen Publications

Library of Congress Cataloging-in-Publication Data
Rayner, Nicholas.
        The jewels of the Duchess of Windsor.
        1. Windsor, Wallis Warfield, Duchess of, 1896–
2. Jewelry—Private collections.   3. Windsor, Edward,
Duke of, 1894–1972.   4. Great Britain—Nobility—
Biography.   5. Great Britain—Kings and rulers—Biography.
I. Title.
DA581.W5R39   1987   941.084'092'4   87–14218

ISBN 0–86565–089–6
Printed and bound in Italy

 Contents

THE COLLECTION AND THE SALE	6
SALE PRICES	18
A ROYAL BIOGRAPHY	20
MEMORABILIA OF THE DUKE	81
DESK SEALS, OBJETS DE VERTU AND SILVER	82
SWORDS, KNIVES, SPORRANS AND REGIMENTAL DRESS	106
JEWELS OF THE DUCHESS	118
SAPPHIRES	130
EMERALDS	148
RUBIES	158
A JEWEL BOX	168
CATS	196
PEARLS	208
DIAMONDS	216

LE PRINCE CHARMANT
RUE DE LA PAIX.

The Collection and the Sale

'The Jewels of the Duchess of Windsor, Lot One.' The atmosphere was electric as the auctioneer opened the bidding for a sale that would prove to be one of the most dramatic and widely followed of all time. One thousand five hundred bidders were packed into the great marquee pitched on the shores of Lake Geneva (Lac Léman). Another 700 were linked by closed-circuit televisions in the Hôtel Beau-Rivage next door. In New York, Sotheby's salesrooms, connected to Geneva by satellite, had been fully booked for weeks. And to inform the rest of the world, 250 journalists and 17 international television crews were reporting the sale live. The astonishing event actually took place in two sessions. The first started at nine o'clock in the evening of 2nd April 1987, and its emphasis was on the Duchess' important jewellery, including several pieces of historic interest marking stages in the emergent romance of Mrs Simpson and the Prince of Wales, later King Edward VIII. That session finished at half-past midnight. The next session, at half-past four in the afternoon of 3rd April, was largely devoted to memorabilia of the Duke, but it also offered several minor, though beautifully designed, pieces belonging to the Duchess. The session finished at nine that evening. Both sales had taken nearly three times longer than normal owing to the extraordinary quantity of bids.

What was the reason for the excitement surrounding this sale? Why was this collection so remarkable? And what could explain the enormous prices generated by the auction?

The Jewels of the Duchess of Windsor attempts to provide answers to such questions, by recounting a bit of the fabled jewels' history and illuminating something of their lore. For these are the jewels and precious objects that illustrated the chapters in the most famous love story of modern times. Already important for their provenance, their distinctive style and the fine quality of their gemstones, the jewels have now been rendered still more legendary by that remarkable auction in Geneva in April 1987, an auction that achieved seven times its pre-sale estimate, raising $45 million for the Pasteur Institute to help in the fight against cancer and AIDS.

A CONNOISSEUR'S COLLECTION

The beauty of jewellery cannot be truly conveyed by photographs, however good the photography may be. The depth of colour and lustre of the gemstones, the weight and subtlety of the mounting can be fully appreciated only from handling and seeing the jewels themselves. Although the illustrations of the Duchess' jewellery on these pages are superb, a true connoisseur would not be able to give a final judgement based solely from the book.

The Duke of Windsor was such a connoisseur. All his life he had a passion for precious stones and jewellery. His love for jewellery probably stemmed from the admiration he held for his mother Queen Mary. A stately presence, George V's Consort wore the Royal Jewels with great elegance and looked magnificently regal when dressed for formal occasions in her garland necklace, or her high pearl choker, and her glittering diadem. Equally magnificent jewellery must have figured in the romantic image the Prince of Wales formed of the lady he would marry one day.

The Duke had been brought up amongst the splendour of some of the greatest houses of England—Windsor Castle, Sandringham, Buckingham Palace—and all were filled with wonderful works of art. Queen Alexandra's superb Fabergé collection gave him an admiration for exquisitely made precious objects. His awareness of the fine quality of the furniture, porce-

lain, silver and paintings that graced the royal residences prepared the Duke to approach everything aesthetic with a critical eye.

The Duke was also interested in the innovative design of his day, an interest that he combined with a keen perception of quality and an enduring sense of colour. In contrast to the conservatism of his father, King George V, the Duke followed and sometimes set the latest trends in fashion. Like all Royal personages who dress for so many different occasions, he was steeped in the traditions of ceremonial wear. This produced in him a critical sense of attire, a subject on which he wrote with authority. The 'Windsor Knot' and the 'Prince of Wales check' passed into style and are now part of the English language.

The Duke himself collected with taste and knowledge. Over the years, he acquired many very fine pieces of English furniture. It was unfortunate that these practically all disappeared without proper recognition in 1973, at the time of the sale of the Moulin, the Windsors' country house outside Paris. The Duke was an expert in snuff-boxes and Russian works of art. He owned several superb boxes, including the famous *tabatière* of Madame de Pompadour, which he presented to the Louvre in the 1960's. His Royal Highness also gave much of his French furniture—it was of royal quality—to the Palace of Versailles. And on a lighter note, he collected his beloved Duchess. According to their close friend, the Countess of Romanones, the Duke had over three hundred framed photographs of her in his small private apartment. 'They were strewn all over his bedroom and even his bathroom,' she recounts, 'on tables, on the walls, his bed was surrounded, in every niche and corner of those two not large rooms.' She continues: 'It seemed curious to me that the pictures were always of the Duchess alone, not accompanied by him; although there were some of her with their favourite dogs, and one of her with her aunt. They were snapshots mostly, perhaps some had been taken by him.'

People who knew the Duke appreciated his knowledge of art. One of his friends, Godfrey Thomas, staying with him at Schloss Enzesfeld in March 1937, wrote in a letter addressed to the Duke's solicitor George Allen, as follows: 'I haven't for many years known my host in such good form or so easy from every point of view. . . . He is more than ever a charming and considerate host; and as a guide round the Kunsthistorisches Museum in Vienna, as good as any professional.'

The Duke of Windsor adored jewellery. He took immense trouble to choose jewels that his Duchess could wear to advantage. This landmark collection, therefore, was formed by a combination of the Duke's appreciation of quality, design and colour and the Duchess' innate sense of fashion and showmanship, which gave the collection a theme that was recognizable throughout its span.

When the Duke of Windsor bought a present for the Duchess, it is doubtful that he ever considered that he was forming what would become one of the most celebrated collections of jewels in the world. The Duke must be given credit for the remarkable choice of those first important items obtained in the latter half of the 1930's. He was known to have spent long hours in the pre-war years with Jeanne Toussaint of Cartier, and with Renée Puissant at Van Cleef & Arpels, both eminent designers in their field. The relationship between these two highly imaginative artists and their Royal client often produced jewels which were still considered avant-garde ten years after their manufacture. The jewels would be the forerunners of the style of the late 1940's, when new designs began to emerge after the war.

Most of the jewels were made in a period when the craft of jeweller was still at its peak. A good setter was considered to be an artist, and the standards of the Parisian mounters and finishers equalled those of their counterparts in St Petersburg earlier in the century. In many instances the gemstones were of outstanding quality, having been specifically selected to meet the demands of the Duke's discerning eye.

A LADY OF FASHION

The lady for whom the Duke and his jewellers worked was elegance personified. The favourite client of Chanel, Schiaparelli and Balmain, she helped to introduce Balenciaga to Paris and counted Givenchy among her personal friends. It was the latter who always insisted that the Duchess bring her latest jewels to his atelier so that he could create a dress as a backdrop to show them off at their best. For thirty years Wallis Windsor was hailed by couturiers and fashion writers both in Europe and America as one of the world's best-dressed women. It was she who effected the choice of the later jewels, thereby influencing the taste of countless others.

The Duchess, like the Duke, took an interest in jewellery design and became the source of some original ideas. One was a zipper necklace made, by Van Cleef & Arpels, of a working zip completely set with interlocking diamonds. It was transformable into two bracelets, but the Duchess later had her diamond zip incorporated in a spectacular evening dress.

The Duchess was not the easiest of clients, a point delicately made by Laurence Krashes of Harry Winston, Inc., the New York jeweller, during a recent BBC interview: 'She was easier on design than she was on price, and she was a terrible stickler on design.' Mr Krashes also remembers the episode of the Indian emerald drop necklace that the Duchess bought from Winston in 1957. Soon afterwards, she wore it at a grand reception to which the Maharanee of Baroda had also been invited. The Maharanee instantly recognized the necklace, with its fine stones, as having been made from a pair of Indian anklets recently sold from the Baroda collection. 'My dear,' she announced to a companion, in a rather loud voice, 'have you seen, she is wearing the beads I used to have on my feet!' The Duchess returned the necklace to Winston the following day.

There appears to be no photograph of the Duchess of Windsor wearing antique jewellery. Her inclination was towards the stylishly decorative jewels of the 1940's and 1950's. These were often extravagant, rather than conservative in taste, creations designed with wide expanses of polished gold, occasionally sprinkled with bombé clusters of emerald, sapphire or ruby beads and highlighted with pavés of diamonds. She was among the first to wear yellow-gold jewellery, which took the place of platinum after 1945. This became a popular fashion in France, partly because gold had been rationed and hence hoarded during the war years. Now there was an urge to show off the yellow metal for so long banned by repressive legislation.

Even without its Royal connection, this extraordinary group of jewellery and precious objects would have been of enormous interest to jewellers and art historians alike. Historical events can be followed through inscriptions on a remarkable number of pieces. In this respect, the Duke himself was following a family tradition. A hundred years earlier, Prince Albert had dates and messages inscribed on some of the jewels he gave Queen Victoria. (Some say that Queen Victoria had a few of the messages inscribed after the fact.) The three ingredients of history, quality and design made the Windsor collection altogether unique.

Although he did not so state in his will, the Duke of Windsor at various times expressed a wish that the jewels be broken up, to prevent their being worn by any other woman after the Duchess' death. Luckily, Wallis Windsor thought otherwise. The Countess of Romanones echoes the sentiments of the Duchess when she asks: 'Would it not have been a pity if this collection had disappeared like the jewels of the widow of a Hindu Prince, on her cremation pyre?' Not only would the design, the history and the love represented by the jewels have been lost, but the funds from their sale would never have been raised to combat the terrible scourges of our day.

The constant stream of valuable gifts that the Duke presented to his wife clearly demonstrates his generosity. The generosity of the Duchess is now reflected in her wish that the recipient of the huge sum of money generated by the auction of her jewels be the Pasteur Institute. The Duke and Duchess of Windsor deeply appreciated the welcome and hospitality they had received from the French Government. The grand house in the Bois de Boulogne was lent to them virtually free of rent, much as a 'Grace and Favour' house would have been lent to a member of the Royal Family in England. By choosing the Pasteur Institute, a very French but internationally famous center for medical research, the Duchess will have benefitted not only the French people, but ultimately the whole world.

THE SALE

As Prince of Wales, the Duke of Windsor had travelled more widely than any other member of the Royal Family before him. The visits to the capitals of the Empire by the Heir to the Throne had been magnificent affairs of pomp and ceremony. Images of glory connected with the Duke remained fixed in the minds of millions of people. His Royal Highness was part of the personal history of countless citizens of the Empire. They or their parents had cheered him through the streets of Montreal, or perhaps had been moved by his speech from Viceroy House in Delhi. And many of them wished to own a little part of this history. Their desires were expressed in the form of order bids, almost a thousand of which were received before the auction, a record amount for a single Sotheby's sale. None of them was successful.

The first indication of the extraordinary interest in the sale was the realization, in mid-February 1987, that the initial run of 15,000 catalogues would have to be reprinted. Thousands of inquiries were flooding into Sotheby's offices throughout the world. From the Argentine to Canada to India, people began to tender their pre-sale bids.

Hundreds of pre-sale bids were also received from the United States, where the Duchess was considered by many a folk heroine—the girl from next door who married a King. The exhibition in New York attracted huge crowds from near and far. So many came to see the jewels that a line of people five deep soon wound its way through Sotheby's extensive galleries on 72nd Street and full block down York Avenue. Police control became necessary, and although viewing groups were timed to fifteen minutes each, many people had to be turned away.

Interest in the event began to absorb the media. Newspapers and television networks kept Sotheby's Press Department busy dispensing information and interviews. It was front-page material in *The New York Times*. 'Nightline', the much-followed American news programme, devoted half an hour to it. And the BBC produced a superb documentary entitled 'The Uncrowned Jewels'. Using a rostrum camera and special techniques for lighting, they obtained some of the best jewellery photography ever put on the screen.

A private exhibition was arranged in Palm Beach at the fabulous Montsorrel Mansion, which was subsequently sold for US $18 million. The marble salons of the sea-side palace formed an apt setting for the jewels. And there was an additional reason for choosing this venue. The Duke and Duchess had often been guests in the house, whose late owner, Mrs Young, had named her largest guest room after the Duchess. The Duke preferred to sleep in a simpler and smaller bedroom attached.

One thousand people were invited to the reception in Palm Beach, and such was the interest that 1,500 accepted and 2,000 came! The guest list was a 'Who's Who' of the rich and famous in America. The guests included many who had known the Windsors and remembered some of the jewels from the time the Duchess had worn them. Present was the cosmetics tycoon Estée Lauder, a long-standing friend of the Duchess and one who shared her taste for yellow diamonds.

In Geneva the scale of things proved less grand, for as one of the New York organizers succinctly explained, the whole of the Swiss city (population 230,000) could be housed in 72nd Street! As the night of the sale approached, the massive marquee grew like a mushroom on the shores of Lac Léman. Sotheby's staff were working night and day to arrange a seating plan that would have defeated experienced booking clerks at Covent Garden, faced as they were with the problem of how to choose between serious bidders and interested spectators. Owing to the number of requests for seats, there was a danger that late-arriving bidders would be excluded in favour of those who only came to watch. An attempt was made to vet requests, but this task called for such delicacy that it would have confounded even the most experienced diplomat.

Left. The jewels were exhibited at Montsorrel, a Palm Beach seaside mansion The Windsors were very much part of the Palm Beach social scene during their early visits to the United States. Right. Marvin Mitchelson, Hollywood's famed divorce lawyer, with a friend for whom he bought one of the Duchess' many necklaces.

When the marquee had been reserved to capacity, the overflow quickly filled up the salons of the Hôtel Beau-Rivage, which was connected by television and telephone link-up systems. There were assistant auctioneers to relay the bidding from each room. The same arrangement was made with Sotheby's York Avenue salesrooms, even though New York was three thousand miles away, and the link-up had to be made by satellite. Thanks to extremely competent communication experts on both sides of the Atlantic, the systems worked perfectly throughout the auction.

In Geneva, at nine on the evening of 2nd April, under the bright arc lights of the television cameras, the great tent was filling with an excited and glittering audience, the men in dinner jackets, the ladies mostly in long dresses, many wearing their best jewels for the occasion. The important international dealers were there to a man—Graff, Gol, Mousseif and Horowitz, to mention but a few. The relevant jewellers—Cartier, Van Cleef & Arpels,

The tent, above, set up on the Quai du Mont Blanc in Geneva. This was but one of many salesrooms. Below. Nicholas Rayner rides happily on a sea of bids from all over the world. The Givenchy models are holding the last lot of the evening sale, a Golconda diamond for which a Japanese dealer paid over $ 3,000,000. Watching are Sotheby's executives, the Earl of Gowrie, previously Britain's Minister of Arts, and Simon de Pury, previously curator of the Thyssen-Bornemisza collection in Lugano, Switzerland.

Harry Winston, Garrard, Fred Leighton—were all represented by their owners or senior directors. Even Verdura was there, in the guise of Ward Landrigen who had recently acquired the business founded by the late Sicilian Duke. Famous people were taking their seats at the front. Easily recognizable were Baron and Baroness Thyssen, Princess Abir Toussoun, Ann Getty, Baroness Edmond de Rothschild, Princess Firyal and Shirley Bassey among them. Hundreds of journalists were noting it all down from the Press enclosure, and television crews were busy filming from side-line platforms for their millions of viewers to see.

RECORD-BREAKING PRICES

'The Jewels of the Duchess of Windsor, Lot One' (ill. 150). The bidding opened to a forest of raised hands. Sotheby's American President, relaying the bidding from New York, was on his feet, shouting the prices as they rapidly increased across the Atlantic. On the other side of the room, the staff were frantically signalling the bids coming from the outlying rooms in the hotel. Several of the staff manning the independent telephone lines were awaiting their chance to enter the fray. The order bids quickly surpassed, prices shot up. Now the bidding was in the tent. Now on the telephone. Now in the hotel against New York. The first lot in an auction is traditionally an item of lesser importance. This ruby and sapphire bead clip had been estimated at a reasonable SF 7,000-10,000, but up went the price, higher and higher, until is was sold, before a stunned Geneva audience, to New York for SF 65,000 (US $43,000; £27,000). The buyer was Alexander Acevedo, who afterwards said that he had been determined to buy the first lot at practically any cost because he had heard that somebody intended to buy the whole collection, lot by lot. His strong bidding discouraged this idea and helped to get the auction off to a fast start.

And so it continued. Estimates were exceeded by as much as five times, even, in some instances, by thirty times. Rarely has any auction been so animated. The three ravishing Givenchy-clad models holding the jewels to be sold stepped onto the stage one by one. A pre-filmed image of each jewel was shown on television monitors scattered throughout the salesrooms. Above the auctioneer there was a giant screen displaying the jewel fifty times life-size. For those not conversant with Swiss francs, two currency converter boards clicked out the prices in five different currencies.

The seventeen television cameras whirred. People in the tent were aware that perhaps three hundred million viewers could be watching at any one time. A sense of theatre in the salesroom is important. The fleeting moment when the spotlight is on the bidder, when necks crane and head s turn, can encourage him to go one more bid, and one more again.

At Lot 15, the Duke's diamond dress suite (ill. 207), the pace of bidding accelerated still further. Offers were being accepted around the SF 50,000 level, when the auctioneer was told that New York had a bid for SF 300,000. As he announced this to the room, the mass of arms waving for attention slowly sank in unison, as if drilled by an instructor. All but one, that is. Mr. Wafic Said was also determined to buy this lot—so determined that he fought the American bidder all the way up and finally beat him at SF 600,000 (US $400,000; £247,000), or 50 times the estimate.

The auctioneers were aware of the tremendous interestf focused on Lot 27, the Prince of Wales plumes (ill. 81). And they knew that a certain film star in California, who had been married to a famous Welshman and who had been a friend of the Duchess of Windsor, would be bidding by telephone. But never did they imagine tha the price would surpass half a mil-

Many royal and international celebrities attended the sale and previews. Top left. Mr Laurence Graff, London's most important dealer in precious stones, with his family. The Graff firm purchased many of the most important stones at the sale. Top right. John L. Marion, Chairman Sotheby's North America greets Mrs Thomas Mellon Evans at a benefit reception for the Pasteur Institute at Sotheby's galleries. Center, left to right, Baroness Edmond de Rothschild, Elizabeth Taylor wearing the Prince of Wales' diamond clip. H.R.H. The Infanta Pilar de Borbon, Duchess of Badajoz, the sister of King Juan Carlos of Spain. Below. Once Sotheby's announced the Windsor sale, the curiosity of the public was unprecedented. A line formed around the entire block on York Avenue for the time that the jewels were on exhibit.

lion Swiss francs. When Elizabeth Taylor eventually won the brooch for SF 850,000 (US $567,000; £350,000), no one was more delighted than she. Later, the actress made a touching Press announcement, stating that although it was the first jewel she would ever have to pay for herself, she was pleased that the price was high since the money would go to such a wonderful cause. Miss Taylor has been for some time a leading light in raising funds to help AIDS victims. The Pasteur Institute, after having been the first to identify the AIDS virus, is now heavily involved in researching a cure for the deadly disease.

The London *Daily Mail* bought several items, including Lot 33 (ill. 98), the gold and gem-set powder compact, as prizes for a quiz competition lasting several weeks. The promotional campaign proved to be immensely popular with readers and sold tens of thousands of extra newspapers.

Marvin Mitchelson, the famous Hollywood divorce lawyer, bought Lot 46 (ill. 155), the amethyst and diamond bib necklace for SF 875,000 (US $583,000; £360,000). Delighted with his purchase, Mitchelson immediately asked Sotheby's to announce that he had bought it in memory of his mother. This the auctioneer did, to the applause of the audience.

Batteries of telephones, manned by Sotheby's staff members, received bids from around the world. These offers competed against bids from the New York salesroom, two outside Geneva salesrooms watching on closed-circuit television, as well as from the packed audience in the tent.

Afterwards, Mitchelson recounted how in the old days his family had lived on Windsor Boulevard in Los Angeles and how his father had always called his mother 'The Duchess'. Further, his late mother had much admired another amethyst necklace belonging to a friend. For all these reasons, Mitchelson was determined to buy this one, which the experts had estimated at SF 24,000. He said that he might possibly have stopped 'this side of SF 2 million.'

Laurence Graff, the London jeweller, who must rank as one of the world's top three dealers in important stones, paid SF 2 million (US $1.3 million; £823,000) for Lot 81, the

Great Mogul emerald (ill. 120). He bought it to give to his wife for their twenty-fifth wedding anniversary. Graff thinks it the finest emerald he has ever seen. The hammer price, with the premiums added, calculates at US $107,500 per carat, which doubles the previous world price paid for any emerald. It is unlikely that the Duke ever bought jewels with a view to investment, but if the Great Mogul's 1936 price of £10,000 is multiplied by 25 to allow for the period's deflation, the gem can be considered to have appreciated about 500 percent.

The auction had lasted four hours, but almost all the hundreds of bidders, spectators, staff, technicians and journalists remained in place, enthralled by auction history in the making. A hush descended on the audience as the drama of a fabulous evening came to its climactic moment in the sale of the final Lot 95: the McLean diamond (ill. 214). The bidding opened to a flurry of raised hands at SF 1 million. In leaps and bounds, with bids being called from New York and the hotel, the price rose quickly to SF 3 million. From there, it became a tense and drawn-out fight between two men: a Japanese gentleman in the Geneva tent and a telephone bidder from North America. The Japanese seemed the more determined, and it soon became clear that the telephone bidder was exceeding his pre-sale mark. At every counter offer, the latter took more time to decide, until the crowd was awaiting each call with bated breath. At SF 4 million even the Japanese hesitated. At SF 4.1 million the telephone bidder deliberated a seemingly endless three minutes before deciding to go one more. The auctioneer waited patiently for a last hesitant bid from the Japanese, and then knocked the item down to Mr. Takagi, for a record of SF 4.3 million (US $2.7 million; £1.8 million). The room burst into cheers of relief from the tension, applauding long and loudly for the generosity of the Duchess of Windsor and the huge sum of money that had been raised for the Pasteur Institute.

Long before this dénouement a pattern had begun to emerge in the sale. The items fetching the most extraordinary prices were those with the greatest sentimental attachment. Lot 31, the bracelet of crosses (ill. 98), with its jewellery value listed in the catalogue at SF 22,000, sold for SF 520,000 (US $347,000; £214,000). Lot 32, the cigarette case engraved with maps and routes (ill. 97) went for SF 400,000 (US $267,000; £165,000), 100 times its pre-sale estimate. In the second half of the sale, premiums paid for nostalgic connections were higher still. Lot 134, a gold pocket watch that the Duke had given the Duchess in 1939 (ill. 100), was valued at SF 5,000 but made SF 700,000, and the Duchess' gold handbag set sold at SF 900,000. But even these added values would be surpassed by items with a close tie to the Royal Family. A little circular photograph frame containing a picture of Queen Mary, which she had given to King George V, sold for SF 620,000, over 1,000 times Sotheby's pre-sale valuation. The Duke's naval sword, given to him by his father in 1913, brought SF 2 million, easily a record price for any sword. His ten desk seals totalled SF 2 million. They and other precious objects from the earlier life of the Duke were bought for Mohamed al Fayed, an Egyptian businessman who owns Harrod's in London and the Ritz Hotel in Paris. Partly because of the millions spent by Mr al Fayed to restore the Ritz to its former classical glory, the French Government had granted him the lease of the Windsors' mansion in the Bois de Boulogne. The new tenant plans to install a museum in most of the house, whose contents he purchased after the death of the Duchess. The world-wide excitement caused by the jewellery sale would suggest that the public's fascination with the Duke and Duchess of Windsor has waned little in the fifty-odd years since the two lovers met. It seems likely therefore that the stately residence in which they lived out their later years is destined to become a traditional stop on the itinerary of many a future visitor to Paris.

Sotheby's Sale Prices
THE JEWELS OF THE DUCHESS OF WINDSOR
Thursday 2nd/Friday 3rd April, 1987

The prices shown are the hammer prices *plus* the 10% buyer's premium. Currency exchange rates used: 2.43 SF = £ 1 and 1.50 SF = $1 US (rounded to the nearer £ or $).

Ill. No.	Estimate Swiss Francs	Swiss Francs	£ Sterling	US Dollars	Ill. No.	Estimate Swiss Francs	Swiss Francs	£ Sterling	US Dollars
1	1,500-2,000	55,000	22,634	36,667	60	8,000-10,000	88,000	36,214	58,667
2	1,200-1,800	99,000	40,740	66,000	61	2,500-3,500	176,000	72,428	117,333
3	1,000-1,500	154,000	63,374	102,667	62	2,500-3,500	110,000	45,268	73,333
4	2,000-3,000	418,000	172,016	278,667	63	1,500-2,500	121,000	49,794	80,667
5	1,000-1,500	418,000	172,016	278,667	64	7,000-10,000	132,000	54,321	88,000
6	1,000-1,500	308,000	126,749	205,333	65	2,500-3,500	275,000	113,169	183,333
7	1,500-2,000	440,000	181,070	293,333	66	1,000-2,000	38,500	15,844	25,667
8	1,200-1,800	308,000	126,749	205,333	67	12,000-15,000	2,200,000	905,350	1,466,667
9	2,000-3,000	418,000	172,016	278,667	68	5,000-8,000	220,000	90,535	146,667
10	2,000-3,000	462,000	190,123	308,000	69	800-1,200	71,500	29,424	47,667
11	2,500-3,000	49,500	20,370	33,000	70	1,200-1,800	55,000	22,634	36,667
12	500-700	38,500	15,844	25,667	71	4,000-6,000	605,000	248,971	403,333
13	500-700	49,500	20,370	33,000	72	1,500-2,500	33,000	13,580	22,000
14	300-400	38,500	15,844	25,667	73	2,500-3,500	77,000	31,687	51,333
15	600-900	99,000	40,740	66,000	74	500-800	27,500	11,317	18,333
16	600-900	110,000	45,268	73,333	75	500-600	11,000	4,527	7,333
17	600-900	143,000	58,848	95,333	76	200-300	33,000	13,580	22,000
18	500-700	110,000	45,268	73,333	77	700-1,000	49,500	20,370	33,000
19	500-700	99,000	40,740	66,000	78	300-500	22,000	9,054	14,667
20	500-700	66,000	27,160	44,000	79	300-600	27,500	11,317	18,333
23	700-1,000	55,000	22,634	36,667	80	1,000-1,500	30,800	12,675	20,533
24	800-1,200	24,200	9,959	16,133	81	500-800	15,400	6,337	10,267
25	2,000-2,500	44,000	18,107	29,333	82	800-1,200	110,000	45,268	73,333
26	2,000-2,500	49,500	20,370	33,000	83	600-800	528,000	217,284	352,000
27	4,000-6,000	242,000	99,588	161,333	84	800-1,200	11,000	4,527	7,333
28	7,000-8,000	66,000	27,160	44,000	85	700-900	27,500	11,317	18,333
29	800-1,200	33,000	13,580	22,000	86	500-800	55,000	22,634	36,667
30	5,000-8,000	110,000	45,268	73,333	87	800-1,000	16,500	6,790	11,000
31	2,500-3,500	33,000	13,580	22,000	88	800-1,000	22,000	9,054	14,667
32	2,000-3,000	77,000	31,687	51,333	90	8,000-10,000	451,000	185,597	300,667
33	300-500	7,700	3,169	5,133	91	500-700	66,000	27,160	44,000
34	700-900	33,000	13,580	22,000	92	22,000-30,000	572,000	235,391	381,333
35	500-700	13,200	5,432	8,800	93	3,000-4,000	77,000	31,687	51,333
36	800-1,200	13,200	5,432	8,800	94	2,000-3,500	198,000	81,481	123,000
37	250-350	11,000	4,527	7,333	95	1,000-1,500	33,000	13,580	22,000
38	450-550	44,000	18,107	29,333	96	4,000-6,000	52,800	21,728	35,200
39	3,000-5,000	154,000	63,374	102,667	97	4,000-6,000	440,000	181,070	293,333
40	2,000-3,000	110,000	45,267	73,333	98	5,000-8,000	176,000	72,428	117,333
41	1,500-2,000	176,000	72,428	117,333	99	1,500-2,000	132,000	54,321	88,000
42	500-600	30,800	12,675	20,533	100	5,000-7,000	770,000	316,872	513,333
43	1,500-2,000	33,000	13,580	22,000	101	30,000-35,000	297,000	122,222	198,000
44	12,000-18,000	385,000	158,436	256,667	102	4,000-6,000	264,000	108,642	176,000
45	600-800	682,000	280,658	454,667	103	3,000-4,000	220,000	90,535	146,667
46	600-800	418,000	172,016	278,667	104	6,000-8,000	275,000	113,169	183,333
47	600-800	550,000	226,337	366,667	105	8,000-12,000	132,000	54,321	88,000
48	10,000-15,000	330,000	135,802	220,000	106	450,000-550,000	1,540,000	633,745	1,026,667
49	8,000-10,000	319,000	131,276	212,667	107	450,000-550,000	1,540,000	633,745	1,026,667
50	2,000-3,000	396,000	162,963	264,000	108	15,000-18,000	220,000	90,535	146,667
51	3,000-4,000	330,000	135,802	220,000	109	6,000-8,000	143,000	58,848	95,333
52	3,000-5,000	242,000	99,588	161,333	110	22,000-28,000	176,000	72,428	117,333
53	500-800	66,000	27,160	44,000	111	2,000-3,000	132,000	54,321	88,000
54	500-800	44,000	18,107	29,333	112	15,000-20,000	99,000	40,741	66,000
55	500-800	49,500	20,370	33,000	113	3,000-5,000	55,000	22,634	36,667
56	2,500-3,500	330,000	135,802	220,000	114	22,000-28,000	143,000	58,848	95,333
57	2,500-3,000	440,000	181,070	293,333	115	140,000-180,000	1,265,000	520,576	843,333
58	8,000-10,000	99,000	40,740	66,000	116	60,000-80,000	440,000	181,070	293,333
59	3,000-4,000	242,000	99,588	161,333	117	10,000-15,000	121,000	49,794	80,667

Ill. No.	Estimate Swiss Francs	Swiss Francs	£ Sterling	US Dollars	Ill. No.	Estimate Swiss Francs	Swiss Francs	£ Sterling	US Dollars
118	60,000-80,000	660,000	271,604	440,000	169	6,000-8,000	93,500	38,477	62,333
119	100,000-150,000	561,000	230,864	374,000	170	8,000-12,000	440,000	181,070	293,333
120	600,000-800,000	3,190,000	1,312,757	2,126,667	171	3,000-4,000	220,000	90,535	146,667
121	200,000-250,000	825,000	339,506	550,000	172	3,000-4,000	165,000	67,901	110,000
122	400,000-500,000	1,320,000	543,210	880,000	173	2,500-4,500	60,500	24,897	40,333
123	70,000-90,000	242,000	99,588	161,333	174	4,500-5,500	30,800	12,675	20,533
124	200,000-300,000	528,000	217,284	352,000	175	4,500-5,500	33,000	13,580	22,000
125	45,000-55,000	231,000	95,062	154,000	176	4,500-5,500	28,600	11,770	19,067
126	7,000-10,000	220,000	90,535	146,667	177	4,500-5,500	15,400	6,337	10,267
127	12,000-15,000	110,000	45,267	73,333	178	20,000-30,000	176,000	72,428	117,333
128	12,000-15,000	132,000	54,321	88,000	179	150,000-200,000	1,540,000	633,745	1,026,667
129	9,000-12,000	60,500	24,897	40,333	180	2,000-3,000	71,500	29,424	47,667
130	150,000-180,000	1,650,000	679,012	1,100,000	181	250,000-350,000	2,090,000	860,082	1,393,333
131	30,000-40,000	220,000	90,535	146,667	182	100,000-150,000	286,000	117,695	190,667
132	1,200,000-1,500,000	3,905,000	1,606,996	2,603,333	185	120,000-150,000	660,000	271,605	440,000
137	550,000-650,000	968,000	398,354	645,333	186	300,000-350,000	1,430,000	588,477	953,333
138	60,000-70,000	275,000	113,169	183,333	187	15,000-20,000	154,000	63,374	102,667
139	60,000-80,000	384,000	158,436	256,667	188	7,000-10,000	220,000	90,535	146,667
140	140,000-180,000	1,210,000	497,942	806,667	189	4,000-6,000	99,000	40,741	66,000
141	4,000-6,000	308,000	126,749	205,333	190	230,000-260,000	1,100,000	452,675	733,333
142	700-1,000	33,000	13,580	22,000	191	25,000-35,000	451,000	185,597	300,667
143	4,000-6,000	165,000	67,901	110,000	192	80,000-100,000	231,000	95,062	154,000
144	1,500-2,000	115,500	47,531	77,000	193	25,000-30,000	275,000	113,169	183,333
145	5,000-7,000	121,000	49,794	80,667	194	4,000-6,000	71,500	29,424	47,667
146	3,000-3,500	77,000	31,687	51,333	195	3,000-5,000	66,000	27,160	44,000
147	25,000-35,000	605,000	248,971	403,333	196	20,000-30,000	77,000	31,687	51,333
148	25,000-30,000	220,000	90,535	146,667	197	5,000-8,000	45,100	18,560	30,067
150	7,000-10,000	71,500	29,424	47,667	198	2,000-3,000	88,000	36,214	58,667
151	4,000-6,000	30,800	12,675	20,533	199	3,000-4,000	35,200	14,486	23,467
152	8,000-12,000	82,500	33,951	55,000	200	70,000-90,000	297,000	122,222	198,000
153	5,000-7,000	71,500	29,424	47,667	201	55,000-75,000	275,000	113,169	183,333
154	900-1,200	330,000	135,802	220,000	202	300,000-400,000	1,320,000	543,210	880,000
155	24,000-28,000	907,500	373,457	605,000	203	700,000-900,000	3,410,000	1,403,292	2,273,333
156		308,000	126,749	205,333	204	10,000-14,000	88,000	36,214	58,667
157	4,000-6,000	170,000	69,959	113,333	205	3,000-5,000	41,800	17,202	27,867
158	35,000-45,000	231,000	95,062	154,000	206	6,000-8,000	176,000	72,428	117,333
159	14,000-18,000	187,000	76,955	124,667	207	12,000-16,000	660,000	271,605	440,000
161	2,000-3,000	88,000	36,214	58,667	208	230,000-280,000	429,000	176,543	286,000
162	4,000-6,000	66,000	27,160	44,000	209	350,000-450,000	506,000	208,230	337,333
163	15,000-18,000	52,800	21,728	35,200	210	4,000-6,000	154,000	63,374	102,667
164	4,000-6,000	88,000	36,214	58,667	211	4,000-6,000	48,400	19,918	32,267
165	2,000-3,000	61,600	25,350	41,067	212	10,000-15,000	66,000	27,160	44,000
166	12,000-16,000	440,000	181,070	293,333	213	550,000-700,000	935,000	384,774	623,333
167	2,000-3,000	165,000	67,901	110,000	214	1,250,000-1,500,000	4,730,000	1,946,502	3,153,333
168	10,000-15,000	990,000	407,407	660,000					

A Royal Biography

Queen Victoria, in a famous photograph of 1894, is seated between her son and grandson, Their Royal Highnesses Albert Edward, Prince of Wales, the future Edward VII, and the Duke of York, later George V. In her arms she cradles the latter's baby son Prince Edward, who is almost lost to sight in a voluminous christening robe of Honiton lace. The Queen subsequently wrote that she had been to the child's christening and afterwards 'we were photographed, I, holding the Baby on my lap, Bertie and Georgie standing behind me, thus making the four generations.'

Ever keenly aware of her family's dynastic responsibilities, the Queen-Empress, although gazing down at her great-grandson with an equivocal expression, radiates matriarchal satisfaction at the arrival of this new-born heir to the throne. Had she the gift of clairvoyance, however, Queen Victoria would have been truly astonished by the course of future events. Not so Keir Hardie, a Socialist Member of Parliament, who in response to a motion in the House of Commons that congratulations on this occasion were due to Her Majesty was of the opinion that from his childhood Prince Edward would be surrounded by sycophants and flatterers and be taught to believe himself as of a superior creation. 'In due course,' he declared prophetically, 'he will be sent on a tour round the world, and probably rumours of a morganatic alliance will follow and the end of it all will be the country will be called upon to pay the bill.'

Prince Edward, known in the family by his last name David, was born at ten o'clock in the evening of 23rd June 1894 at White Lodge, Richmond Park, the home of his maternal grandparents, the Duke and Duchess of Teck. His mother, Princess Victoria Mary (May), a great-grandchild of George III and later Queen Mary (ill. 6), originally had been selected by Queen Victoria in 1891 as the most suitable bride for her grandson Prince Albert Victor who, after his father the Prince of Wales, was in direct line of succession. Not long after the announcement of their engagement, however, the Prince, then serving as an officer in the 10th Hussars, suddenly died of pneumonia. The grief of the Prince's parents and relations, though real, was partially assuaged by some feeling of slight relief, for it had become clear that neither in health nor in temperament was he equipped for the exalted position in which his birth had placed him. But his passing, while apparently solving one problem, caused another related to the future of his brother, Prince George: Whom should *he* marry? Princess Victoria Mary remained the appropriate candidate for wife of an heir to the throne; so, despite any feelings of embarrassment, their marriage was arranged in due course.

Happily for the couple, the Duke and Duchess of York, as they became known, were well suited, remaining genuinely devoted to one another until his death over forty years later.

A famous photograph by W. & D. Downey of Queen Victoria with three future British monarchs united for the Christening of Prince Edward in 1894. The Queen wrote in her diary, 'We were photographed, I, holding the Baby on my lap, Bertie and Georgie standing behind me, thus making the four generations.'

He wrote to her at the start of their marriage that he 'adored' his 'sweet May', while she, confiding in her old governess, confessed that 'Georgie is a dear . . . he adores me which is touching,' adding, 'I feel as if I had been married for years and quite settled down.'

As a wedding present in 1893, the Prince of Wales gave them a house called York Cottage on his Sandringham estate in Norfolk. Although too small despite having been extended on several occasions, this 'glum little villa', as Sir Harold Nicolson described it, became their home, and it was here that they and their growing family spent much of the next seventeen years. The house's narrow passages were cluttered with royal pages and footmen, and the lady-in-waiting was obliged to sleep in a noisy cubicle adjacent to the pantry. Here Prince Edward's brothers and sister were born between 1895 and 1905: Albert George, later King George VI; Mary, the Princess Royal; Henry, Duke of Gloucester; George, Duke of Kent; and, lastly, John.

These children, in common with many of their privileged contemporaries, were brought up by servants in virtual isolation from their father and mother, both of whom have been much criticized for their failure as parents, and who in their separate ways were wholly unsuited to fill that responsibility. The two eldest Princes, particularly, stood in awe of them, an awe that sprang partly from the sense of royalty that the Duke and Duchess, taking their predestined roles excessively seriously, allowed to influence their every action.

A highly developed reserve and shyness are attributes by which Queen Mary will be remembered. It was thought furthermore, even by those who knew her well, that she had no maternal feelings at all. Her husband, both early on and later as George V, tended to place himself at a superior remove from his sons, which as they grew older opened up between himself and them feelings of unease and disaffection. This became unpleasant to Prince Edward, subsequently recounting that nothing like the summons, 'His Royal Highness wishes to see you in the Library,' could be 'so disconcerting to the spirit.' These interviews, while sometimes of the kindliest nature, were often called to deliver a rebuke for 'being late or dirty, for making a noise on some solemn occasion, or for wriggling and scratching in church.' And so the son's often imagined misconduct was to incur the father's displeasure for the remainder of the latter's life.

Parental demonstrations of affection were rare. Both the Princes Edward and Albert George, the two eldest boys, were of nervous dispositions; when they visited Queen Victoria they rewarded her approaches by bursting into tears. 'Gangan', as they called her, found this behaviour decidedly irritating, perhaps not realizing that the children were terrified in her stately presence. Nevertheless, on her eightieth birthday she presented Prince Edward with a silver-framed photograph of herself as a keepsake (ill. 47). If the Queen, her Indian servants and her curious revolving cabins wherein she habitually took her breakfast, worried the Prince, he suffered no such inhibitions with his grandparents, the Prince of Wales, later Edward VII, and his wife, Princess Alexandra.

There being but a year between them, Prince Edward and Prince Albert grew up and were given an education of sorts together. A room in York Cottage was fitted up as a schoolroom, and Mr Hansell, a keener golfer and yachtsman than a scholar, was appointed their tutor. From him they learnt little else besides an appreciation of nature in long walks through the local woods. The boys were never introduced to, perhaps were even discouraged from learning about, music, literature and the arts. Instead, their father was determined they should master the gun and become good horsemen. If this life sounded dull for the Princes, especially without companions of their own age, then it was not always so, particularly on their

White Lodge in Richmond Park, above, was the home of the Duke and Duchess of Teck, the maternal grandparents of Prince Edward. It was here that he was born on 23rd June, 1894. Center left. Prince Edward of York, later King Edward VIII, at the age of two and a half in 1896. Center: a family portrait of Prince Edward with his parents Queen Mary and George V. Center right. Prince Edward of Wales in a sailor suit photographed in 1903 with his favourite brother, Prince George, later Duke of Kent. Below. Prince Edward of Wales, later King Edward VIII (back right), photographed in 1910 with his brothers and sister, the Princes Albert George, subsequently King George VI, Henry, George and John, and Princess Mary.

visits to the Big House at Sandringham when their grandparents, King Edward VII and Queen Alexandra, were entertaining (ill. 41). Their fondness for Prince Edward was fully reciprocated. Going to see them one day, he ran over to his grandfather, past parents and servants, to kiss him on hands and cheek again and again.

Lord Esher, writing in 1906 of Prince Edward when not yet twelve years old, observed that he 'develops every day fresh qualities, and is a most charming boy; very direct, dignified and clever. His memory is remarkable....' Little wonder then that this 'alert and sensitive' youth left home soon afterwards in some trepidation, tears drenching his new blue uniform, to start a career at the Royal Naval College at Osborne on the Isle of Wight. His father, who accompanied him that day, 2nd May 1907, managed to still his worries with tales of his own early days in the Navy, pressing into his hand a silver pocket watch inscribed: 'For dear David from his affectionate Papa.'

Here at Queen Victoria's Italianate 'marine villa', given to the nation by Edward VII, the Prince mingled for the first time with other boys besides his brothers and some of the children on the estate at home in Sandringham. As a newcomer he was asked by another cadet for his name. 'Edward', was the reply. 'Edward what?' 'Just Edward.' But this reference to his royalty was unusual, and he joined in the life of the College with enthusiasm, even to the extent of once having a pot of ink deliberately spilled down his neck. Also because he was not large in stature he became known familiarly by his peers as 'Sardine', a nicely chosen pun on the name of Wales (whales)!

In May 1909 Prince Edward transferred to Dartmouth College, where after two years he was to complete his five years of naval training. His much loved grandfather King Edward VII died on 6th May, whereupon, amid much private and public sorrow, his father ascended the throne as George V, and Prince Edward himself became Duke of Cornwall as well as Heir Apparent (ills. 39 and 40). For his sixteenth birthday on 23rd June 1910 the Prince was summoned to Windsor Castle to stay with other members of the Royal Family before being confirmed the next day by Dr Randall Davidson, the Archbishop of Canterbury (ills. 42 and 51). It was on this occasion, too, that the King conferred upon him the title of Prince of Wales.

Writing in his diary on 22nd June 1911, the day before his seventeenth birthday (ill. 59), the Prince began, 'Papa and Mama's Coronation Day. Papa rated me a Midshipman,' the latter commemorated by a medallion inscribed with the date and the legend 'God be with you' (ill. 38). Of the ancient ceremony at Westminster Abbey the Prince wrote: 'I had to go & do hommage [sic] to Papa at his throne, & I was very nervous....' For his part the King confided in his diary that he nearly broke down when 'dear David' came to do homage, as it reminded him of 'when I did the same thing to beloved Papa.' State visits by the King and Queen accompanied by Prince Edward and Princess Mary followed to Ireland, Scotland and Wales, the pageantry culminating for the Prince with his investiture as Prince of Wales at Caernarvon Castle early in July. Sensitive to what his naval friends would think, he very much objected, as any young man might, to the 'fantastic costume' of 'white satin breeches and a mantle and surcoat of purple velvet edged with ermine' with which he had to be fitted for the occasion. His father was adamant that it should be worn, saying that he should not take a mere ceremony so seriously. Queen Mary managed to settle the Prince's qualms by convincing him it was for the best.

The new Prince of Wales, as he stated later, discovered something of himself then when he realized his own recoil 'from anything that tended to set me up as a person requiring hom-

Sandringham.

age.' This telling expression of feelings has been seen by some as a forewarning of the unhappy climax of December 1936. But for the moment the King was pleased with his son's public performance and appearance in Wales, realizing at the same time that recent events had been emotionally exhausting for the boy. He therefore arranged for him to take a three months' sea voyage as a midshipman on the battleship *Hindustan*, joining at Cowes in August 1911 (ills. 35 and 38). It was apparently at this time that the Prince commenced to smoke, a habit in which he took considerable pleasure for the rest of his life.

No sooner had the Prince come home to York Cottage than the King, in one of those daunting Library interviews, advised him that for the sake of his education he was to travel for four months to France before returning to England, where he was to go up to Oxford. That winter of 1911/12, while his parents were away in India, the Prince stayed on at York Cottage with his sister and two youngest brothers under the eye of Mlle Dussau and Mr Hansell. In response to a letter telling his father of his prowess at shooting on the estate, the King, commenting acidly, 'there can't be much game left,' wrote in castigation that he was not riding or hunting enough: 'If you can't ride, you know, I am afraid people will call you a duffer.' Nevertheless, this interlude proved valuable; the two Princes, Edward and George, found that a real friendship more than just brotherly love had sprung up between them.

Travelling as the 'Earl of Chester', a not very convincing pseudonym, the Prince of Wales set out for Paris in the spring of 1912 with Finch, his valet, and Mr Hansell to stay with an old friend of his grandfather's, the Marquis de Breteuil. Here the Prince tasted a luxury denied him at home in having an entire suite to himself. He met many interesting people at the de Breteuils' weekly luncheons, and he made a number of friends among his younger acquaintances, who took him to swimming and tennis parties and introduced him to fast cars. He also played golf, went riding and attended the races. During his sojourn in France

the Prince was recalled briefly to Windsor for his eighteenth birthday, an occasion that he seems to have remembered chiefly for the fact that his father allowed him to smoke. Smoking, particularly in public, he thought, gave him more self-assurance. That in the event of the King's death he could now have gained full regal powers without a regency apparently did not occur to him. Returning in the autumn from France, where his tutor, M. Escoffier, had learnt more English than he had French, the Prince stayed at Balmoral. Lord Esher wrote of him at this time: 'It is a charming mind–grave, thoughtful, restrained, gentle, kindly, perhaps a trifle obstinate and sober for so young a lad.' The same authority observed that the Prince, who did not think himself 'a bit above the average,' was still devoted to the Navy, speaking at length of his friendly relations with the officers and men and 'how he loved to talk with the men of their homes and their pleasures and their troubles.' This attractive quality, enlarged over the years by a show of concern for his father's subjects both at home and abroad, became one that so long as he remained Prince of Wales earned him great popularity. His charm and that of his own personal appearance, his sudden smile and fair, youthful good looks, added further to the enthusiastic reception he received everywhere he went. Yet he was known by intimates as being moody, one even remarking: 'Of course, he was very spoilt.'

By October 1912 the Prince found himself in residence at Oxford, where he attended Magdalen College (ill. 15). He was accompanied again by his old tutor and valet together with a recently appointed equerry, Major the Hon. William Cadogan. However much young Edward might try, the academic life of Oxford was not much to his liking. Instead he began at last, through Cadogan's suggestion, to take a real interest in riding and hunting. The Prince was bold and courageous in his new enthusiasm, a matter noted with satisfaction by the King.

The Prince attended Magdalen College at Oxford in 1912, but remained at first rather separated from his fellow students. He is seen here marching to camp.

Oxford at first unnerved the Prince, encouraging a shyness that forced him to keep to his rooms for fear of being stared at by the curious, especially tourists. He eventually relaxed and began to enjoy himself, even to the extent of practicing the banjo at all hours until his neighbours at Magdalen mounted a good-natured protest.

The Easter and summer vacations of 1913 found the Prince of Wales in Germany, where he had gone to learn about its people and to improve his mastery of their language. He was well received, not as in France by friends but by members of the various royal houses to whom, for the most part, he was related. His first host was his uncle King Wilhelm of Württemberg, from whom it seems likely he received on 8th April an enamelled silver cigarette case (ill. 13). Before leaving Germany the Prince paid a courtesy visit on Kaiser Wilhelm II, like his father a grandson of Queen Victoria, whom he found at his desk seated rather disconcertingly upon a block mounted with a saddle complete with stirrups.

Characteristically, the Emperor's uniforms, worn in a succession of ever more splendid outfits, dazzled the young Prince, whose own fascination for the sartorial, both ceremonial and informal, was by this time, despite earlier doubts, already highly developed. Indeed, he and the King, who was equally interested but who was very conservative in his taste, were often in sharp disagreement on the subject. In sarcastic tones, George V asked one morning of his son, who had just entered the room for breakfast: 'Is it raining in *here?*' What he meant, of course, was that one should turn up one's trousers in that absurd manner *only* when crossing puddles.

Uniforms, of which the Prince of Wales was entitled to wear many, were incomplete without their accoutrements, and it was in March 1913 that as a Royal Navy Lieutenant he received from the King a Royal Naval officer's sword made by Wilkinson's of Pall Mall (ill. 67). The Duke of Windsor's collection of such items, including military buckles, buttons and the like, are evidence of his abiding obsession for the ceremonial in dress, despite his protestations to the contrary. In this, however, he was not nearly as well informed as his Uncle Arthur, the aging Duke of Connaught.

The Prince's final term at Oxford passed quietly enough, although the King wished him to become more involved in the royal duties. On 13th June 1914, therefore, he was present at St Anselm's Church on the Duchy of Cornwall estate in South London to give the only speech since his first public utterance at Caernarvon three years earlier. In the course of the year George V recalled him twice to Windsor Castle to meet visiting foreign royalty. He was expected on these occasions to practice, in his own words, 'the subtle art of talking to the right people about the right things.' Dressed in uniform, the Prince began to form his own opinions about the ceremonial, the extravagant hospitality that, so different from the life of an undergraduate, he found excessive, 'rot & a waste of time, money, & energy.' Little knowing what was to befall them in a few months, the Prince while staying at Windsor was introduced by his father to that 'elegant couple' the Archduke Franz Ferdinand, Heir Apparent to the Austro-Hungarian Empire, and his morganatic wife.

The import of the Archduke's assassination at Sarajevo on 28th June was not at first generally appreciated, least of all by the handsome young Prince who had just celebrated his twentieth birthday. Grown up now, he had lost his former shyness and was able to jot in his diary on 10th July after three nights of dining and dancing: 'I've had no more than 8 hrs. sleep in the last 72 hrs.!!' By the end of the month his mood had changed; he was 'very depressed' having heard on the 31st the news of Belgium's mobilization. 'All this is too ghastly,' he wrote, '& that we should be on the brink of war is almost incredible....'

War was declared at the beginning of August, whereupon the Prince applied to his father for an Army commission in the hope of seeing active service. A few days later he was gazetted to the Genadier Guards, posted to the 1st Battalion at Warley Barracks, Essex, and as a special honour despite his small size (5 ft. 7 in.) detailed to the King's Company. The Prince's joy was soon turned to frustration when in mid-September he was transferred from the 1st to the 3rd Battalion upon the former being sent overseas. A terrible blow to his pride, he remonstrated with the King, who told him it was the decision of the Secretary of State for War, Lord Kitchener. Not to be put off, the Prince insisted on an interview with Kitchener, telling him it didn't matter if he was killed: 'I have four brothers.' But that was not the point; Kitchener could not allow the possibility of the young man being taken prisoner. Eventually, however, the Prince as usual got his way, and on 16th November 1914 he left for Northern France to be attached to the staff of Field-Marshall Sir John French, Commander-in-Chief of the British Expeditionary Force.

Nevertheless, what proved to be a job of paperwork in a safe position was not the Prince of Wales' idea of active service. Not to be convinced that he was useful by just being who he was, particularly when impressing the French Generals, he continually agitated for more stimulating duties. These he was given, and firstly in May 1915 was moved to the General Staff of 1st Army Corps near Béthune, from where he was able to visit the front on many occasions. Several other postings followed during which the Prince became widely known both in the trenches and at home for his concern for the men and his unflagging physical vigour and courage. 'A bad shelling will always produce the Prince of Wales,' his brother officers are supposed to have said. Six weeks' leave early in 1918 saw him briefly in London, where he met and fell in love with Freda Dudley Ward, 'a pretty little fluff' according to Lady Cynthia Asquith, whose husband was a Whip in the Liberal Party. The Prince afterwards returned to France to serve as a Major in the Canadian Corps, remaining with them until the end of the war. Then for a short period he was with the Australian Corps in Belgium, before coming home in February 1919, happy that the conflict was finally over but, like everyone of his generation, thoroughly disillusioned.

In November 1918 the King received a letter from the Prince of Wales wherein he read of his son's thoughts on the 'epidemic of revolutions' sweeping through 'the enemy countries which certainly makes it a hard & critical time for the remaining monarchies.' The Prince had no doubt that the British monarchy was safe, but 'of course it must be kept so & I more than realize that this can only be done by keeping in the closest possible touch with the people.... I'm sure you won't mind when I tell you that I'm out the whole of every day seeing & visiting *the troops* i.e. "*the people*"!!!!' The King's pleasure at learning of these sentiments was tempered by worries concerning his son's new-found ability to mix with all manner of people in a way impossible for any previous Prince of Wales. 'You must always remember your position and who you are,' the King told him upon the eve of the next phase in the Prince's career. A goodwill tour had been suggested by Prime Minister Lloyd George, who realized that a personal appearance by the popular young Prince of Wales in various countries of the British Commonwealth would do much to strengthen the bonds of Empire, which at that time showed signs of weakening. As the Canadian Government had already approached George V on this subject, it was quickly decided that the Prince should leave for that country with a promise to the other Dominions that visits to them would follow in due course.

The now immensely popular Prince of Wales was much in demand in the various countries of the Commonwealth. His first trip was to North America in 1919, commencing with an extended visit to Canada where he bought a cattle ranch at Calgary. He is seen, overleaf left as 'Chief Morning Star,' dressed up to please the local Indian population, and also paddling a canoe on Lake Nipigon in northern Canada. The Prince was impressed with the informality of the New World, but not so with the ceremonial of state occasions which he found onerous.

The Canadian tour, with a short visit to the United States of America included, lasted from August until December 1919. Tens of thousands welcomed the Prince on his first afternoon in Quebec, and similar scenes of enthusiasm were the rule everywhere he went. The Canadian Pacific Railway put a magnificent train, a veritable travelling hotel with room enough for his staff, at the Prince's disposal (ill. 31). A platform at the rear of this vehicle allowed His Royal Highness to give the many spontaneous speeches which the people gathering at each stop demanded. At home his parents were at once gratified and horrified by the popularity of their son's progress. The King confessed that 'it makes me very proud of you . . . ,' while Queen Mary wrote from Balmoral that her 'head almost reels at the amount you are doing & I feel angry at the amount of handshaking and autograph writing you seem com-

pelled to face!' The handshaking started, it is said, when a man in the crowd thrust forward saying: 'Put it right here, Ed. I shook hands with your grand-dad.'

New York at the end of the tour made a great impression on the Prince. The most abiding memory of the city was not the grand welcome he was given but, not unnaturally for a lively twenty-five-year-old, a visit to the *Ziegfeld Follies*, where he heard John Steel singing 'A Pretty Girl Is Like a Melody' surrounded by a tableau of the most glamourous beauties on earth. With this vision in mind, the Prince sailed on H.M.S. *Renown* for England. For two and a half months at the start of 1920 he managed to find time for many sporting engagements, including a much-publicized game of squash with Captain Eric Loder, Master of the Pytchley Hunt, who had married a Gaiety Girl, as well as a demanding series of public duties. Then on 16th March, taking a tearful leave of his friend Mrs Dudley Ward, the Prince boarded the *Renown* once more for a tour of New Zealand and Australia, which occupied his time until the following October.

According to those most close to him, the forty-six thousand miles of the tour, the more than two hundred places visited and the countless people met left the Prince feeling totally exhausted. Indeed in Australia he had first shown that the pressures of such a ruthlessly demanding public life were not always to his liking. Lord Louis Mountbatten, his cousin and travelling companion, remembered that beneath the smile and despite the fun they had had, the Prince 'was a lonely and sad person, always liable to deep depressions.' In accordance with earlier promises, Lloyd George now wished him to leave relatively quickly for India, a plan endorsed by the King, who himself had travelled there in 1905, as had his father before him in 1875. But the Prince, longing for a rest, managed to get this new tour deferred until the following autumn; he was frankly delighted to be able to spend an uninterrupted year at home.

Notwithstanding public appearances in many parts of the Kingdom, the Prince led a full private life, subsequently recalling that 'the 1921 London season was one of the gayest in my memory.' He also took up fox-hunting and began to ride at point-to-point meetings. At

In later years, New York City became a second home to the Duke of Windsor. Above. On his first visit as Prince of Wales to New York, the social highlight of the year, he is welcomed to City Hall by Mayor John F. Hylan in early 1920. Below. Point-to-point racing, an extremely dangerous sport, was taken up by the Prince of Wales upon his return from Australia. Although he was considered a poor rider, he felt compelled to demonstrate his courage but a number of well publicised falls gave the King and Prime Minister cause for concern. Later, during George V's illness of 1928/29, Queen Mary succeeded in persuading the Prince to give up what had become his favourite recreation.

33

India was the jewel of the British Empire: the Durbar at Bombay in 1911, when King George V and Queen Mary were crowned Emperor and Empress of India, marked the very apogee of Imperial splendour. Their son, the Prince of Wales followed them to the sub-continent in 1921, where, in spite of some local trouble caused by followers of Mahatama Gandhi, he was warmly received. He was splendidly entertained by high-ranking Indians who took him tiger shooting (above) or, like the Maharaja of Patiala (below), pig-sticking. After the latter expedition, his Royal Highness was photographed with prizes of the hunt together with his host and Captain Edward Dudley Metcalfe, soon to become one of the Prince's closest friends.

one of these, with the Pytchley Hunt at Great Brington on 16th March 1921, he won a silver-gilt cup by riding one of his own horses called 'Rifle Grenade' (ill. 48).

Once more joining H.M.S. *Renown*, the Prince of Wales and his staff set out from Portsmouth for India and Japan on 26th October 1921 (ills. 12 and 91). They reached Bombay on 17th November, where the Prince was welcomed by the Viceroy, Lord Reading, several splendidly attired Maharajas and Nawabs and a great mass of people who on the state ride in a horse-drawn carriage showed their pleasure by 'an immense murmur of delight' and handclapping. Despite partially successful agitation by the followers of Mahatma Gandhi and the Congress Party, the tour was generally a success, the crowds of India accepting the Prince among them in 'an ecstasy of enthusiasm.' In addition to such public appearances, the royal visitor was privately entertained on a magnificent scale. Early in 1922, for instance, he stayed with the thirty-year-old Maharaja of Patiala, a potentate who lived in a pink palace a quarter of a mile long employing several thousand domestics. John Lord has written of a morning when Patiala provided hog-hunting, which ended 'with all the Prince of Wales' five pigs laid out in attitudes of extinction . . . for a souvenir photograph with Prince and Maharaja in the pose of conquerors.' Afterwards dinner was served on a spectacular silver dinner service especially imported from London at a cost of £30,000.

The visit to India was also made memorable for the Prince by his introduction to the young Indian Cavalry officer, Captain Edward Dudley Metcalfe, known to his friends as 'Fruity', with whom he remained on intimate terms until the latter's death many years later. Metcalfe shared with the Prince an interest in many things, including clothes and horses, but above all he became a favourite companion because of his 'gaiety and good humour.' In 1925 he married Lady Alexandra Curzon, a daughter of Lord Curzon of Kedleston.

The exhausting tour of India and the Far East over, the Prince returned to England at the end of 1922. His round of social events in London and the country and his many public

King George V in 1923 riding to hounds, a favourite sport, with his sons, the Prince of Wales and the Duke of York.

engagements were quite as numerous as they had been the year before. Riding to hounds and steeplechasing became recreations in which he revelled, although his share of mishaps and spills attracted widespread publicity precisely because he was the Prince of Wales. Neither the King nor Ramsay MacDonald, the first Labour Premier, was silent when in 1924 he fell from his mount during a race for Lord Cavan's cup. Concussed, the Prince lay senseless for half an hour and was afterwards confined to bed for nearly a month.

Later that year the Prince travelled for his own pleasure to the United States, where he was initially drawn by the international polo matches between Britain and America, which were to be played on Long Island. As had become usual by now, he was joyfully received, and the wealthy owners of private estates there vied with one another to provide the most elaborate entertainment. The American newspapers were full of reports, some exaggerated, about the Prince's every movement and his breaking engagements because of the late hours he kept. The King confronted his son with them on his return home, opining that such visits to other countries were worthless if all they did was to produce vulgar stories about the heir to the throne. Looking back many years later, the Duke of Windsor was in no doubt that what most puzzled his father about him was his continued state of bachelorhood. The Prince had no doubt he would marry one day but in his own time and to someone of his own choice.

The Prince's fourth and last official tour took place during 1925, when on 28th March he left for Africa and South America, returning on 16th October. At home once more, the Prince's seemingly endless attendance at banquets and other similar proceedings confirmed his dislike of such ceremonial, which he referred to privately as 'the decorated circus.' Besides these, he was left very much to himself, having no other official business to attend to. The Prince therefore interested himself in various ex-servicemen's organizations and with efforts to alleviate the conditions of the poor and unemployed. Because he was debarred by his station in life from politics, the events surrounding the General Strike of 1926 and his inability to play any part in it proved particularly irksome.

The year 1927 was noteworthy for two foreign trips that the Prince took with his brother Prince George. During the second, a return visit to Canada, the Prince of Wales was for the first time brought into intimate contact with the new Prime Minister, Stanley Baldwin, and his wife, Lucy. Before long the two men were to be involved in a great constitutional crisis, the immediate cause of which was a young American woman whom the Prince had yet to meet. At that moment, however, she was living quietly at Warrenton in the state of Virginia, awaiting a divorce from her first husband, Lieutenant Earl Winfield Spencer, an aviator in the United States Navy.

George V's health, which of late had not been robust, suddenly deteriorated in the winter of 1928. His eldest son was away in Africa, a trip taken mostly for pleasure during which

B essie Wallis Warfield, the future Duchess of Windsor, born at Blue Ridge Summit, Pennsylvania, on 19th June 1896, with her mother, Alice Montague Warfield, left and at the time of her marriage in 1919 to Lieutenant Earl Winfield Spencer, right.

he played golf and indulged in big-game hunting. Despite becoming ill for a while with malaria and on one occasion being charged by an infuriated elephant, the Prince was so enjoying the relative freedom of life in the open air that he began to wonder how anyone in similar circumstances would wish to return to civilization. But a message reached him in the bush bearing bad news of the King's condition. In one of the provincial headquarters several days later the royal party learnt that the King had had a relapse. The Prince was thus advised to return to London as soon as possible. Part of the hectic journey homewards across Europe was taken in Mussolini's own train. On the way the Prince read a letter dated 6th December from his brother Bertie about their father's state of health, ending: 'There is a lovely story going about . . . that the reason of your rushing home is that in the event of anything happening to Papa I am going to bag the Throne in your absence!!!! Just like the Middle Ages. . . .' The Prince arrived at Buckingham Palace five days later to find his father still very weak and awaiting an operation.

While the King was making his slow recovery, a Council of State was formed to conduct State business in the Sovereign's name. This responsibility fell upon the Queen, her two eldest sons, the Archbishop of Canterbury, the Prime Minister and the Lord Chancellor. It was a worrying time, and Queen Mary, seizing the opportunity to speak to the Prince on a matter that had been of concern to the King for a long time, asked him to give up steeplechasing. In any case, she argued, his increasing public duties necessitated such a move. Reluctantly the Prince observed his parents' wishes, thereby, in his own words, abandoning 'the one pursuit that gave outlet to my competitive spirit.' Having to sell all his horses, he turned increasingly to golf for recreation.

A service of thanksgiving for the return of George V's health, even though the King was far from well, was held at Westminster Abbey in July 1929. By the following January the monarch's condition was sufficiently restored for the Prince to be able to take a trip lasting nearly four months in Africa. This time he was there to shoot big game not with rifles but with a motion-picture camera, his new obsession. Now thirty-five years old, the Prince returned in April 1930 in a mood to lead a more settled life nearer, if possible, the English countryside. He was fortunate therefore to find that Fort Belvedere, a somewhat neglected 'Grace and Favour' house on the Windsor Estate, had become vacant. The King agreed to let him have it, for 'those damn week-ends, I suppose,' and the Prince enthusiastically set

Deciding in 1930 to lead a more settled life, the Prince of Wales moved into Fort Belvedere, a 'Grace and Favour' house on the Windsor Estate, where he held many week-end parties and induged in strenuous gardening, a favourite form of recreation. The Fort became the centre of what was to become a legendary romance.

about transforming the eccentric little castellated Gothic mansion, originally built in the eighteenth century but since enlarged, into a comfortable modern residence. Mrs Dudley Ward, who had been with the Prince when he first saw the house, assisted with the internal alterations. It suited him in several ways, not least that it was secluded, and the garden, like a wilderness after years of uncultivated growth, offered the opportunity to indulge in strenuous exercise (ill. 125).

Over the next six years the Prince was to spend his happiest hours at the Fort. The week-ends would almost always find him there, usually in the company of a select group of friends. One week-end at the start of 1931, however, he was away with Lady Furness at her husband's country seat, Burrough Court at Melton Mowbray, Leicestershire. It was here on Saturday 10th January that the Prince met Mr and Mrs Ernest Simpson for the first time. They had been included on the guest list at the last moment in place of Lady Furness' sister, Consuelo Thaw, a friend of the Simpsons, who had had to rush to Paris where her mother-in-law lay dangerously ill. The daughters of an American Foreign Service officer, Consuelo Morgan and her younger twin sisters Thelma and Gloria had all made 'brilliant' society marriages, to, respectively, Benjamin Thaw, the First Secretary of the United States Embassy in London, Marmaduke Viscount Furness, and Reginald Vanderbilt II. Gloria became the mother of the legendary Gloria Vanderbilt of today. All three of the 'Miraculous Morgans' would play roles in the great drama of Wallis Warfield Simpson and Edward Prince of Wales.

Ernest Aldrich Simpson was born in 1897 in New York, the son of an English father and an American mother. His father, a successful businessman who derived his wealth from shipping, provided a catholic education for his son: trips to Europe during the holidays and ultimately a place at Harvard University. When he was twenty-one Ernest Simpson decided to take up British citizenship, subsequently crossing the Atlantic in 1918 to be gazetted as Second Lieutenant in the Coldstream Guards. Married in 1923 for the first time, he and his wife had a daughter, Audrey, but the relationship was not a happy one, and the couple decided upon a divorce after only three years. In the meantime Mr Simpson, back in New York, had met through mutual friends, Jacques and Mary Kirk Raffray, Wallis Spencer, the estranged wife of Earl Winfield Spencer. Although a frequent visitor to the city, she was then living at Warrenton awaiting her own divorce, which was made absolute on 10th December 1927. Ernest Simpson, then on the point of leaving America to take up a position in his father's London office, immediately suggested that they should become man and wife.

Wallis Spencer at first demurred for although admiring Ernest Simpson for his 'high qualities of mind, stability of character, and cultivation,' she was not sure that her 'Southern temperament was exactly suited to such a man.' Later, however, while staying with friends, Herman and Katherine Rogers at their villa, Lou Viei, near Cannes in the South of France, and suffering from loneliness, she wrote to Simpson to tell him of her change of mind. They were married in London on 21st July 1928, she wearing a yellow dress and blue coat from Paris. The couple at first rented a house in Upper Berkeley Street near Marble Arch before taking a nearby flat, at 5 Bryanston Court, George Street. It was here they were living when the invitation came from Lady Furness to meet the Prince of Wales.

That week-end in Leicestershire turned out to be cold, damp and foggy. The fog was so dense on the first day that the Prince, attired in loud-checked tweeds, arrived with his brother Prince George rather late. The Simpsons were already there, she feeling very far from her best and sniffling with a head cold. Mrs Simpson had been dying to meet the Prince of Wales ever since arriving in London; thus, she was as bright as possible, years later remembering the impression he made on her: 'the slightly wind-rumpled golden hair, the turned-up nose, and a strange, wistful, almost sad look about the eyes when his expression was in repose.' After returning to Bryanston Court, Mrs Simpson wrote to her Aunt Bessie, Mrs D. Buchanan Merryman, to say what a treat it had been to meet the Prince in such an informal way.

It is doubtful whether Mr and Mrs Simpson looked upon their introduction to the Prince as any more than a chance encounter; another would naturally have been most gratifying. For his part the Prince seems also to have enjoyed the week-end but looked upon it as nothing out of the ordinary. Immediately afterwards his attention was taken by the semi-official trip he was about to make to South America to open the British Empire Trade Exposition at Buenos Aires. Part of his time was devoted to a private effort to win back for Britain her dominance in trade there, which had lately begun to drift into the hands of other countries. Interestingly in his autobiography *A King's Story*, the Duke of Windsor specifically mentioned his disappointment at finding that the inexpensive jewellery once exported to Latin America from Birmingham was now largely replaced by less conservative merchandise from Czechoslovakia.

Against a background of deepening economic depression, more than two and a half million out-of-work and hunger marches, the Prince reappeared in England after four months' absence. Ramsay MacDonald's Labour Government, itself in crisis, was replaced that summer of 1931 by a National Government, a coalition. Busy as always on his royal travels across the country, the Prince of Wales made particular efforts, as he had done in previous years, to visit the most despairing areas. He saw many lines of unemployed men, witnessed much misery, all of which appears to have affected him deeply. Raising funds and stimulating the work of voluntary bodies were his best contribution to this unhappy situation, and under his influence the National Council of Social Service set out in January 1932 to assist the indigent and their families.

Times may have been bleak, but the parties and the night-life continued, especially in London. Ernest and Wallis Simpson, mainly through her skill as a hostess, began to attract a regular group of friends and acquaintances to dinner and cocktail parties. She was becoming quite well established. Writing to her Aunt Bessie on 28th April 1931, Mrs Simpson boasted of the fact in a recital of recent activities, continuing: 'May 6 I'm having Lord & Lady Sackville, Lady Milford Haven, Lady Fitzherbert, Tamar [Consuelo Thaw] and Mrs Vanderbilt with men for dinner and bridge.' Now at the age of thirty-five and after all the years of uncertainty, she was suddenly making a success of her life.

Mrs Simpson as a child, then Bessie Wallis Warfield, born at Blue Ridge Summit, Pennsylvania, on 19th June 1896, was to learn that her father and mother, Teackle Wallis Warfield and Alice Montague had been married against their respective families' wishes. Their wedding day was 19th November 1895, but thirteen months later he was dead of tuberculosis at the age of twenty-seven. Warfield's death coming so soon after an ill-advised marriage left his widow and daughter in an awkward situation, with little money and no position. The Montagues were as old and as well-connected in Baltimore as the Warfields, but as their wealth had been dissipated, Alice Warfield could expect no help from her own family. Instead she and Bessie Wallis went to live with old Mrs Warfield and her unmarried eldest surviving son, the banker Solomon Davies Warfield (Uncle Sol), to whom they looked for an irregular allowance. Mother and daughter subsequently went to live with Alice Warfield's elder sister Mrs Merryman (Aunt Bessie), for whom Wallis, as Bessie Wallis preferred to be called, formed a deep and life-long attachment. Afterwards Wallis and her mother moved into a flat of their own, where they were obliged to supplement funds by entertaining paying guests. Mrs Warfield, whose gaiety and good humour under adversity her daughter would always remember even after her death in 1929, sent Wallis to the best schools she could afford, while holidays were spent on the country estates of more fortunately placed relatives.

Worries over money matters temporarily evaporated when in 1908 Mrs Warfield married again. Wallis, then twelve, was sent to Oldfields, a fashionable girls' boarding school, where she was expected to learn, in the words of its motto, 'gentleness and courtesy.' She was happy and popular there, making a number of friends, the closest of whom was Mary Kirk, who would later introduce Wallis to Ernest Simpson. Although Wallis' stepfather died when she was nearly seventeen, her mother, whose finances were once more in a precarious state, was determined to launch her as a debutante in the forthcoming season of 1914/15. Wallis, never exactly beautiful, nevertheless managed to give the impression that she was attractive by sheer force of character. Like her mother, she was vivacious and had already achieved a certain poise and elegance. The coveted invitation duly arrived to Baltimore's Bachelors' Cotillion, an appearance at which was all-important in a girl's search for a suitor. Several young men afterwards called upon Wallis, whose lively manner at the ball had caused a good deal of comment, but nothing came of these light attachments. On a holiday in 1916, however, she was introduced to the dashing Earl Winfield Spencer whom she fell in love with and married that November.

Much had therefore passed in the life of Wallis Simpson by the time she and her second husband came to live at Bryanston Court. Their meeting with the Prince of Wales, even if it could not be repeated, was the necessary fillip to social aspirations that had first been encouraged in Mrs Simpson by her mother all those years before in Baltimore. The Prince meanwhile had returned from South America at the end of April 1931, and his homecoming was marked by a party in his honour given by Lady Furness to which Ernest and Wallis Simpson was invited. Looking over towards the latter, the Prince is supposed to have whispered to Thelma Furness: 'Haven't I met that lady before?' He then moved across to where the couple were standing to say how nice it was to see them again and that he remembered meeting them at Melton Mowbray. The Simpsons were justly proud of this flattering mark of attention.

Less than three weeks later and after much persuasion from her friends, Mrs Simpson was presented at Court wearing a borrowed outfit: Tamar Thaw's white satin dress and Lady Furness' white satin embroidered train and feather and fan. For the occasion, she told Aunt Bessie: 'I am buying an aquamarine & crystal ornament and large aquamarine cross to wear around the neck.... These I need not add are imitations but effective.' Judging from the photograph by Bertram Park of her in this Court dress, Wallis Simpson must have looked enchanting as she swept to the floor in a deep curtsy before Their Majesties the King and

Queen, the Prince of Wales and the Duke of Connaught. That evening the Simpsons joined a small party at Lady Furness' where they found the Prince among the guests. He stayed but briefly, leaving the house to motor to the Fort for an early morning start on the garden. Although Mr and Mrs Simpson lingered on a while after bidding the Prince goodnight, they happened to find him outside by his car, whereupon he offered them a lift to Bryanston Court. On the short journey he chatted amiably about renovations at the Fort. Then, declining Mrs Simpson's invitation to join them in their flat for a nightcap, he said before driving off: 'If you would be so kind as to invite me again, I'd like to do so.' 'That was how it all began,' she was to recall, 'to lead in five short years to a terrible conclusion....'

Some months elapsed before the Prince of Wales and Mr and Mrs Simpson found themselves in each other's company again. Meeting at Tamar Thaw's birthday party just before Christmas 1931, the couple asked the Prince and Lady Furness to dine at Bryanston Court with Mrs Thaw and other friends, an invitation they were glad to accept. Everything went well, the Prince congratulating Mrs Simpson on her American menu, even asking her for the recipe for raspberry *soufflé*. He was also struck by her 'deft and amusing' conversation, her interest in affairs of the moment and her cover-to-cover reading each day of the four leading London newspapers. But above all he admired Mrs Simpson for her forthrightness. 'If she disagreed with some point under discussion,' he wrote in this autobiography, 'she never failed to advance her own views. . . . That side enchanted me.' Furthermore, the Prince was surprised when one evening she begged him to tell her more of his work with the National Council of Social Service. She was curious to learn what a Prince's working day consisted of in a manner no one had ever before dared ask the heir to the throne.

In return for their hospitality, the Prince and Lady Furness welcomed Ernest and Wallis Simpson in January 1932 to one of their informal week-end parties at Fort Belvedere. Mrs Simpson on this, her first, visit was captivated by the place and the charm of its master, whom she found at one moment romping with his two Cairn terriers, Cora and Jaggs, at another wielding a machete for cutting the dense undergrowth in the grounds, and at yet another in the drawing room practicing the needle-point that he had learnt from his mother. Almost nine months passed until the Simpsons received another invitation to the Fort. Their lives in the meantime were beset by niggling financial and domestic problems and her bad health, which somewhat restricted their movements. They nevertheless did take a short business trip to Tunisia and another, only partly business, on the Continent accompanied by Aunt Bessie from America. Busy as usual with his formal duties during the first months of the year, the Prince spent most of August, September and October away in Scandinavia and the Mediterranean.

Friendship between Lady Furness and Mrs Simpson grew during 1933, the one inviting the other with or without her husband a number of times down to the Fort. Besides the Prince himself, Prince George, 'Fruity' Metcalfe and other close friends were also present. It has been suggested that as the Prince's interest in Lady Furness began to wane so she endeavoured to avert his attention by surrounding him with stimulating acquaintances, among whom she counted Wallis Simpson. That the Prince was happy in the latter's company was made clear by his acceptance of further invitations to Bryanston Court, also by the party he threw to celebrate her thirty-seventh birthday on 19th June 1933 at Quaglino's, a smart Jermyn Street restaurant. Mrs Simpson reciprocated a few days later when on 23rd she sent him a small 'presy' for his thirty-ninth birthday.

The Simpsons' continuing financial distress in 1933, exacerbated by poor trading in the shipping business, was so acute that at one point they contemplated leaving the flat in Bryanston Court. Aunt Bessie however came to the rescue, sending 'an influx of cheques' in November. Otherwise the year was a good one; Mrs Simpson's diary had been full, meeting at parties or dining with all sorts of interesting people from the Diplomatic Service, old friends from America and even the stage and screen stars Noël Coward and Maurice Chevalier. Christmas that year was especially lively. She received a gift of three antique rings from Thelma Furness and, from the Prince, a table for the drawing room, which she had chosen herself. Later, in the month of January 1934, Lady Furness sailed for the United States, to be with her twin sister Gloria Vanderbilt during the notorious court trial for the custody of young Gloria, but not before telling Mrs Simpson: 'I'm afraid the Prince is going to be lonely. Wallis, won't you look after him?'

'We have inherited the "young man" from Thelma,' wrote Mrs Simpson to her aunt from the Fort on 12th February: 'He misses her so that he is always calling us up and the result is one late night after another—and by late I mean 4 a.m. Ernest has cried off a few. . . .I am

sure the gossip will now be that I am the latest....' Gradually the Prince felt his affection for Wallis Simpson deepen (ill. 94 [2]), and at Eastertime he quietly broke off his relationship with Lady Furness when, surrounded by stories of her friendship with the young and wealthy Prince Aly Khan, she returned from America (ill. 125). Within a matter of weeks he also ceased to see his old flame Mrs Dudley Ward.

Mrs Simpson naturally found the heir to the throne's attention 'rather thrilling,' telling her Aunt Bessie that if her husband raised any objection 'I shall give the Prince up at once.' But such a course, as the months passed and the Prince's company became more irresistible, would prove difficult indeed.

July 1934 found Wallis Simpson expecting the arrival of her aunt over from America for a short stay just as Ernest Simpson was about to leave on another business trip. Under the circumstances she felt she had to decline an invitation from the Prince to join him and some friends on holiday at Biarritz. But he characteristically brushed aside her excuse saying that both she *and* Mrs Merryman should come (ills. 94 [4, 6], 97, 98). The holiday was a great success, for the Prince a happy interlude before the marriage on 29th November of his favourite brother the Duke of Kent to Princess Marina of Greece (ills. 11, 92 [9] and 93 [3]). To mark the event King George V and Queen Mary held a reception a few days before at Buckingham Palace to which Wallis Simpson, wearing a simple gown designed by Eva Lutyens and a hired tiara from Cartier, and her husband were invited. It was to be the only time Their Majesties were ever to meet their eldest son's future bride.

By tradition the King and Queen and their immediate family spent the festive season at Sandringham, that of 1934 being no exception to the rule. The Prince had not left London however before delivering in person a pre-Christmas present to Mrs Simpson in the form of an 'adorable' Cairn puppy, Slipper, whom they nicknamed 'Mr Loo' (ill. 145). For Christmas itself she received 'a lovely pin with 2 large square emeralds....' Not surprisingly perhaps the New Year of 1935 brought the first sign of a rift between Mr and Mrs Simpson when they were asked by the Prince to accompany him and friends to Kitzbühel in the Austrian Tirol for winter sports. She went alone, Ernest Simpson having stated his desire not to go and emphasizing the point by banging his bedroom door on the night the invitation arrived (ills. 21, 97 and 98). In fact a coolness grew up between them, which continued even after her return to London. It was from this time that the knowledge of Wallis Simpson's friendship with the Prince began circulating widely in society. Before long she was asked regularly to luncheons and dinner parties by several distinguished hostesses who, like Lady Colefax, a well-known interior decorator, and Emerald, Lady Cunard, introduced her to many men and

The official photograph by Bassano taken at the time of the wedding of the Duke of Kent to Princess Marina of Greece on 29th November 1934.

women of the day. The world's press agencies, too, especially those with connections in the United States, began to show great interest in Mrs Simpson, although for the moment Fleet Street maintained a discreet silence.

The Silver Jubilee Celebrations of 1935 to mark King George V and Queen Mary's twenty-five years' reign dominated the social calendar that year. A service was held at St Paul's Cathedral on 6th May (ill. 45), and the next night the Prince of Wales gave a reception at Buckingham Palace for twelve hundred guests (ill. 207). Ernest and Wallis Simpson were asked to the State Ball at the Palace on 14th May, 'a thrilling thing' she confided to her aunt: 'The Prince danced with me after the opening one with the Queen. . . .' In her autobiography *The Heart Has Its Reasons* the Duchess of Windsor recalled of this moment that the King, only a few days away from his seventieth birthday, frail and in failing health, let his eyes rest searchingly upon her. 'Something in his look,' she wrote, 'made me feel that all this graciousness and pageantry were but the glittering tip of an iceberg that extended down into unseen depths . . . filled with an icy menace for such as me.'

June birthdays, Mrs Simpson's thirty-ninth, the Prince's forty-first (ills. 92 [8], 93 [1], 94 [11] and 207), were followed by a summer holiday in the South of France and Austria, again without Ernest Simpson who was away in America (ills 21, 92 [6], 93 [2], 97 and 98). The party included old friends: Lord and Lady Brownlow, Lord Sefton, Colin and Gladys

Buist, Sir John Aird, the Prince's equerry since 1929, and Mrs Evelyn Fitzgerald, another London hostess, the sister-in-law of Lord Beaverbrook. At Cannes they met among others Elsie Mendl, celebrated in American society and, like Lady Colefax, a decorator. Returning home in October, the Prince was convinced that he wished to share his life with Mrs Simpson (ill. 93 [2]). He now began to demonstrate his love for her by lavish gifts of jewellery, the subject of much society gossip, such as the emerald and diamond bracelet by Cartier with which he commemorated that unhappy Christmas of 1935 (ill. 124). Unhappy because it was

A portrait by Cecil Beaton, left, of Emerald, Lady Cunard, the famous London society hostess. Right. Lady Mendl, the former Elsie de Wolfe, in another Beaton photograph, was a well known hostess in pre-war America. She was among those whom the Prince and Mrs Simpson met on their summer holiday in the South of France during 1935. Like her London counterpart, Wallis Simpson's friend Lady Colefax, she was also celebrated as an interior decorator.

the last of George V's life, and the family gathering at Sandringham was full of foreboding. Old inhibitions prevented both the King and the Prince from speaking frankly to one another about their separate fears – the King's for his son's future with Mrs Simpson, the Prince's for his future without her. The Prince could have quoted to his father the line from *Hamlet*, 'She's so conjunctive to my life and soul,' but regrettably he did not.

'After I am dead,' George V had warned Stanley Baldwin, his Prime Minister, 'the boy will ruin himself in twelve months.' But the King was wrong in one important respect; it took less than a year for Edward VIII, who acceded upon the death of his father on 20th January 1936, to renounce the throne.

On the morning of 21st January Edward VIII left the scene of his father's deathbed at Sandringham and flew southwards to perform his first duty as the new Sovereign by appearing before the Accession Privy Council at St James's Palace. As soon after the meeting as possible he telephoned Mrs Simpson sounding 'very tired and overwrought.' While reading that morning's newspapers and listening to radio bulletins, she had recognized the hopelessness of her situation, perceiving the impenetrable barriers of tradition that had already begun to close around her friend, the new Monarch. She was therefore delighted to hear him ask if she would like to see his proclamation. Her affirmative answer secured a window seat overlooking Friday Court, St James's, where Garter King of Arms, the Heralds and attendants

The Silver Jubilee celebrations of 1935 to mark the twenty-fifth anniversary of the reign of King George V and Queen Mary were the most important social events of the year and the occasion of magnificent ceremony. Below. The Lord Mayor presents a pearl-mounted sword to the King at Temple Bar; above, Their Majesties kneel in prayer in St. Paul's Cathedral.

King George V died at Sandringham on 20th January 1936. King Edward VIII, left by aeroplane early the next morning to perform his first duty as the new Sovereign by appearing before the Accession Privy Council. Acutely aware of his new responsibilities and showing signs of stress, the King and his brother, the Duke of York, accompany their father's body.

were to perform the ceremony. To everyone's amazement, not least to Mrs Simpson's and to Alan Lascelles' and Godfrey Thomas', his Assistant Private Secretaries, the King suddenly joined his party. He simply wished to see himself proclaimed, he announced. Peering through the window, they were photographed by a newsreel cameraman, and within the week the British public caught their first fleeting glimpse of Wallis Simpson.

Yet for the moment the public had eyes only for their new King, as popular now as ever he had been during his more than twenty-five years as Prince of Wales. His father had been loved and respected, but Edward VIII offered hope for the future, his charm, his youthfulness, his instinct for reform—all pointed towards a promising new reign. As the King's favourite, Wallis Simpson for various reasons found her life, already hectic, thrown headlong

into a confusion of conflicting emotions, which almost inevitably had an adverse effect upon her health (ill. 92 [4]). On the one hand she was inundated with yet more invitations and flattering correspondence, and on the other she felt isolated in the knowledge that her marriage to Ernest Simpson was coming to an end, and that the King had made it plain to her alone that he intended to make her his wife. Indeed, aside from his formal duties, which were now very numerous, the King continued to see a great deal of her, calling more and more upon her time and support. After six draining weeks, however, she sought, much to the King's irritation, a few days' respite, going to Paris with her friend Mrs Erskine ('Foxy')

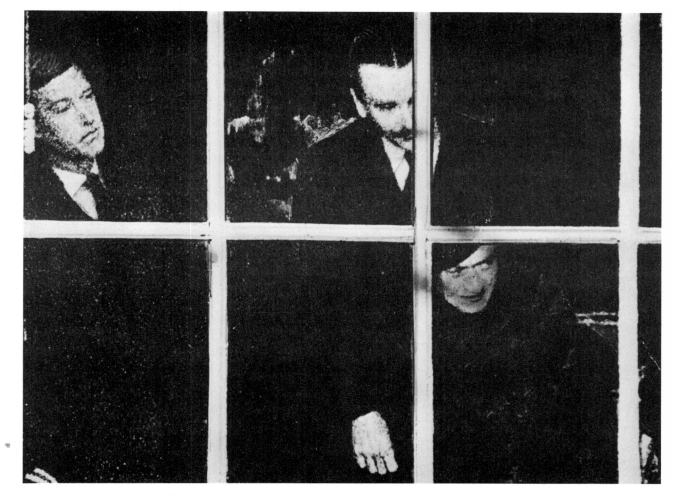

Gwynne, subsequently Countess of Sefton. Mrs Simpson's well-known sense of humour came into play when shortly after her return she presented the King with a gold cigarette case. Inside she had engraved a verse appropriate to the moment, Eleanor Farjeon's 'King's Cross' from *Nursery Rhymes of London Town*, originally published in 1916 in the 29th March issue of *Punch* (ill. 92 [5]).

While she was away, the King and Mr Simpson are supposed to have met to discuss their respective roles concerning Wallis. Ernest Simpson's involvement with another woman had become clear to his wife as long ago as the previous October upon his return from America. Whether he divulged this fact to the King is not known, although it seems likely that he did, because immediately after their conversation Mr Simpson joined his wife in Paris, presumably to talk the whole matter over. The Other Woman was Wallis Simpson's old school friend, Mary Kirk Raffray, who now in March 1936 suddenly announced her imminent appearance in England. Even though Mrs Simpson took the news coolly, it was arranged that she and the King would invite her husband and Mrs Raffray down to the Fort for the week-end of 27th March, four days after the latter's arrival. The Buists and Walter T. Prendergast were also present (ill. 54). No other record of the week-end's events is preserved, beyond that it was the occasion of the King's gift to Mrs Simpson of a most sumptuous jewel: the 'Hold Tight' ruby and diamond bracelet from Van Cleef & Arpels (ill. 137). As if to stress the sentiment, more rubies and diamonds were forthcoming for her fortieth birthday, 19th June 1936, in the form of a dazzling necklace, its mount dated and touchingly inscribed in a facsimile of Edward VIII's hand: 'My Wallis from Her David' (ill. 132).

'Hold Tight' is a phrase whose significance is not hard to divine. It is at once a reference to the function of the bracelet's clasp itself and to emphasize the donor's expressed desire to wed his sweetheart. It must be, moreover, a plea to the recipient to prosecute her idea regarding her marriage with Mr Simpson. 'Divorce I am not planning at the moment,' Wallis Simpson declared to her Aunt Bessie on 4th May in a letter full of implicit reasons why she *should* separate from her husband. A few days later on 11th May she wrote again to tell that 'she [Mrs Raffray] and Ernest stayed up most nights alone until 5 or 6 a.m. and finally went off quite calmly for three days in a hired motor.' But Mrs Simpson's tone of outrage seems to have been counterfeit, perhaps to spare the older woman's sensibilities regarding the pace at which matters were proceeding. Mr Simpson and Mrs Raffray's romance had already forced Mrs Simpson, in her own words, 'to face up to what both Ernest and I had long known. Even the outer shell of our marriage had disintegrated.' After discussing the matter with the King, she approached George Allen, the King's solicitor. He in turn transferred the case to Theodore Goddard, who in future acted upon Mrs Simpson's behalf.

During the first three or four months of his reign these intricacies of private affairs combined with the demands of public life to place the King under intolerable emotional strain. Members of his household, particularly those closest to him, for the most part an older generation of men whose loyalties lay with the sober ways of George V, began to complain. But why Edward VIII chose to keep so many of his father's staff remains a mystery. They found their Sovereign unpunctual, negligent, headstrong, and most of all he lacked consideration by working at odd moments, sometimes deep into the night at hours convenient only to himself. He furthermore steadfastly refused to discuss the fact of Mrs Simpson with his advisers, a topic that became more urgent to them as 1936 wore on. In public the King appeared as before, urbane and charming, except on a few notable occasions, as when in July he did nothing to disguise his weary expression, captured for all to see by a newsreel photographer during a presentation of debutantes at a Buckingham Palace Garden Party. There seems to have been little disquiet at large however, as the King fulfilled his usual heavy schedule of engagements, including the ancient Ceremony of the Maundy at Westminster Abbey in April (ills. 36 and 125). Indeed, the nation's relief expressed in acres of newsprint at their Sovereign's deliverance from a would-be assassin on 17th July confirmed and increased his enormous popularity (ill. 92 [2]).

In accordance with a Fleet Street tradition concerning the Royal Family's personal affairs, British newspapers maintained a discreet silence about Edward VIII's attachment to Mrs Simpson, so much so that to the vast majority of people her name was unknown until word of a possible abdication broke early in December. The foreign press on the other hand had not hesitated for months past to publish a considerable volume of material on the matter, particularly with regard to Wallis Simpson's earlier life. Now, through the couple's 'extraordinary folly and lack of ordinary good sense,' Marie Belloc Lowndes' phrase in which she

King, but not crowned, Edward VIII occasionally allowed himself to appear bored and distracted at public functions as at a Buckingham Palace Garden Party when the season's debutantes were presented. He caused much ill will by leaving before the end of the proceedings.

expressed her opinion of their entire conduct, the King and Mrs Simpson gave the world's reporters an unparalleled opportunity of eavesdropping on their private life.

As Prince of Wales, Edward VIII had been in the habit of spending his summer holidays abroad, and now that he was King he saw no reason for deviating from 'this agreeable and enriching practice.' Overcoming problems relating to the international political situation, the King decided on a vacation in the Eastern Mediterranean aboard a hired yacht, Lady

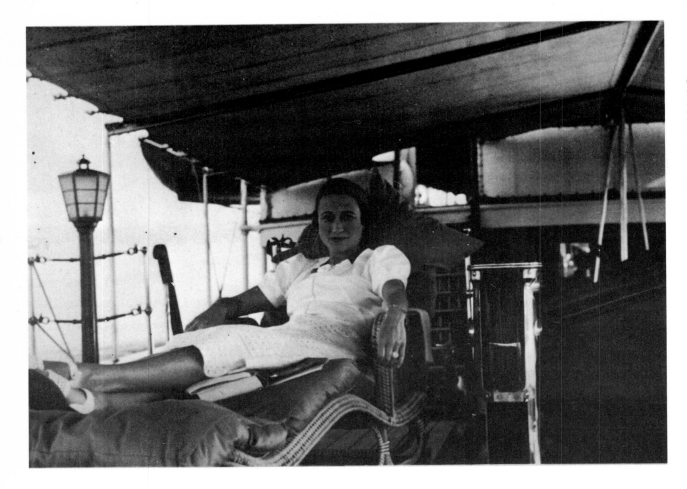

As Prince of Wales, King Edward VIII often spent his holidays abroad. Wishing to continue this tradition now that he was King, he hired Lady Yule's yacht, the *Nahlin,* for a Mediterranean cruise with Mrs Simpson and a group of friends. The cruise caught the attention of the international Press who followed the King and Mrs Simpson whenever they set foot on land. Above. Mrs Simpson on a rattan chair, below, the King works on a jig saw puzzle with Katherine Rogers.

Yule's *Nahlin* (ills. 97 and 98). Unlike Lady Brassey's idyllic transglobal voyage in the *Sunbeam* sixty years before, this cruise proved neither entirely agreeable nor enriching. The original plan had been for the King and his party to join the vessel at Venice; instead, they boarded her at Sibernik in Yugoslavia, where briefly they had been the guests of Prince Paul. At the point of embarkation the King was unexpectedly surrounded by a huge good-natured crowd of smiling, laughing, shouting people who showed as much interest in him as they did in his companion. The international Press, particularly its American segment, had been largely responsible for arousing the mass enthusiasm. 'That should have been a warning to David and me,' the Duchess of Windsor recalled in 1956. 'It meant that our feelings had ceased to

Guests on the Nahlin Included Lady Diana Cooper photographed, right, in the 1920s by Curtis Moffat and Man Ray, and her husband, the Cabinet Minister, Duff Cooper. Left, Katherine Rogers. Wallis Simpson and the King pose for a photograph on the Adriatic coast.

be our private secret; they were becoming the property of the whole world. . . .' Regarding a remote spot they visited on the way, Mrs Simpson bemoaned to her aunt the fact that 'the local militia had to be called out to deal with the crowd. Naturally it ruins exploring and closely resembles the Pied Piper.'

Of those who were the King's guests, Lady Diana Cooper, the wife of Cabinet minister Duff Cooper, has provided the most vivid account, but she and her husband left the *Nahlin* at Athens. Here Helen Fitzgerald and others remained with their host and Mrs Simpson, to be joined by Lord Sefton and Mr and Mrs Herman Rogers. The cruise continued until 6th September, when at Istanbul the King called upon the Turkish President, Kemâl Atatürk. Subsequently boarding the Orient Express the party headed northwards overland, visiting Vienna and elsewhere on the way home (ills. 21, 97 and 98).

In a volume of his memoirs, *The Wandering Years*, Cecil Beaton remembered once viewing some of the Rogers' private cinematograph films, which included episodes of life on the *Nahlin*. 'The King, with Wallis Simpson at his side . . . ,' he wrote, 'seemed a wizened little boy, distinguished by untidy golden hair and a brown, naked back.' Such a response to these fond images shown to a select few was as nothing compared with that to the photographs and reports which now appeared daily in newspapers and magazines worldwide. Suffice to say, as Sir Henry Channon remarked at the time, 'The Mediterranean cruise was a Press disaster. . . .'

Prime Minister Baldwin, who had been away recuperating from the stress of office, was so shocked and preoccupied by what he read on his return to London on 12th October that he begged his incredulous Foreign Secretary, Anthony Eden, 'not to trouble me too much with foreign affairs just now.' The King, too, was appalled, fearing for Mrs Simpson the publicity that would now surely be attracted by her divorce proceedings soon to be heard at Ipswich. A few days before the event he met with Lord Beaverbrook, the influential proprietor of the *Daily Express*, and obtained a gentleman's agreement that led to the case being reported with the utmost discretion. On 27th, the day of the hearing, Mrs Simpson was awarded a decree nisi. Leaving the court afterwards, she was guided through a throng of journalists to return immediately to London, where she was greeted by the King as his fiancée (ill. 120). Mrs Simpson subsequently took a house in Cumberland Terrace, where she was joined by her aunt Mrs Bessie Merryman, who arrived from America aboard the *Queen Mary* on 9th November.

Reluctant at first to talk with his Sovereign about the latter's deepening friendship with Mrs Simpson, Prime Minister Baldwin had meanwhile conferred with Alexander Hardinge, the King's Private Secretary, who arranged an interview at the Fort on Tuesday 20th October. The Prime Minister had been initially disturbed when in June Mrs Simpson was mentioned in the *Court Circular* as a guest, significantly unaccompanied by her husband, at one of the King's small dinner parties at York House. This fact alone had been made much of in the American newspapers. But when Baldwin, prompted by Hardinge, had finally admitted to himself the full implications of the situation, in particular the likely outcome of Mrs Simpson's forthcoming divorce, he saw no reason for further hesitation. As he approached the Fort at ten o'clock that Tuesday morning, crunching up the drive in a diminutive black motor, the King was at the door to greet him. The Prime Minister, very agitated, startled his host by requesting a whisky and soda. After complimenting the King on the beauty of the

Fort's garden, Baldwin settled down to the real subject of his visit. About an hour later, Baldwin departed after being assured by the King that he was indeed most serious in his intentions towards Mrs Simpson.

The political career of Stanley Baldwin had been sufficiently eventful for his subsequent inaction to be variously judged. Some thought it was a sign of ineptitude, others an indication of his perfidious nature. But he was actually just playing for time; it would, after all, be impossible for the King to marry Mrs Simpson and remain on the throne. As Baldwin watched, so the situation generated its own momentum. In America on 26th October, the day before the divorce hearing at Ipswich, William Randolph Hearst's New York *Journal* published an apparently authoritative article stating for the first time that the King had every intention of marrying Wallis Simpson. Also on 26th a long letter from an Englishman resident in the United States, ominously signed 'Britannicus in Partibus Infidelium,' arrived on the desk of Geofffrey Dawson, editor of *The Times* of London. Although Dawson was unable to publish the piece, with its reference to the 'poisonous publicity' accruing in America for Britain and its Monarchy from the news of Edward VIII's relationship with Mrs Simpson, he immediately delivered copies of it to Hardinge at Buckingham Palace and to Stanley Baldwin. Not surprisingly, the Prime Minister counselled continued Press restraint. Whether Hardinge passed the letter to the King is not known, but given his position as Private Secretary, it would have been surprising if he had not.

The first two weeks of November 1936 found the King busy upon state affairs. On 3rd, for the opening of Parliament, he tactlessly cancelled the traditional procession to Westminster because of poor weather; the waiting crowds stood soaking in the rain merely to witness Edward VIII slide through the streets in a sleek limousine. Armistice Day on 11th was followed by a highly successful visit to the Fleet at Southampton. 'He seemed to know personally every officer and seaman,' wrote Sir Samuel Hoare, the First Lord of the Admiralty,

Geofffrey Dawson, left, editor of the Times. Right. King Edward VIII and Queen Mary on their way to Whitehall for the Armistice Day ceremony on 11th 1936, just thirty days before his abdication.

who also remembered that when a rating proposed three cheers for the King, 'there followed an unforgettable scene of the wildest and most spontaneous enthusiasm.' Returning to the Fort, the acclamations of the Navy still fresh in his mind, the King delayed bathing to read a letter marked 'Urgent and Confidential'. Dated that same day, 13th November, it was from Alexander Hardinge who wished to convey certain unwelcome facts that, he stressed, he knew to be accurate. The British Press, Hardinge declared, would not maintain its silence indefinitely about the King's friendship with Mrs Simpson; also the Prime Minister and senior members of the Government were meeting to discuss the increasingly serious situation. In view of these developments, the writer concluded, it was necessary, in order to avoid a political crisis, for Mrs Simpson 'to go abroad *without further delay.*'

The letter shocked and angered the King as much for its 'cold formality' as for its content, behind which Edward VIII thought he sensed a Baldwin plot. Writing fifteen years later, the Duke of Windsor maintained that 'the startling suggestion that I should send from my land, my realm, the woman I intended to marry' was unthinkable. Furthermore, he continued: 'If the real intention was to try to induce me to give Wallis up by pointing at my head this big pistol of the Government's threatened resignation, they had clearly misjudged their man. . . . Only the most faint-hearted would have remained unaroused by such a challenge.' The King lost no time in contacting the well-respected barrister Walter Monckton, an old Oxford acquaintance, who agreed thereafter to become his new intermediary with the Government.

When Mrs Simpson was shown the letter on 15th November two days after its arrival she was stunned, telling the King that it would be best if she followed Hardinge's advice. 'You'll do no such thing,' he announced, 'I won't have it. . . . On the Throne or off, I'm going to marry you.' This was the first time he had mentioned abdication to her, and she was horrified. Bursting into tears, Mrs Simpson told the King it was madness to talk of such a thing. According to her memoirs, she afterwards reproached herself for not leaving England im-

The Abdication Crisis and Parliament, as Prime Minister, Stanley Baldwin outlined the ramifications of a morganatic marriage, the solution most favoured by the King and Mrs Simpson. In closing, he said, 'I cannot conclude this statement without expressing our deep and respectful sympathy with His Majesty at this time.' These sentiments were shared by millions of people throughout the world.

mediately. 'I should have realized that this was the fateful moment,' she wrote, 'the last when any action of mine could have prevented the crisis. What kept me from going? The answer to that hinges on a misconception on my part and, I suppose, the fundamental inability of a woman to go against the urgent wishes of the man she loves.' 'The misconception,' she observed, 'sprang from my failure to understand the King's true position in the constitutional system.'

Baldwin called for the second time upon Edward VIII at the latter's insistence at Buckingham Palace on the evening of Monday 16th November. During their conversation he explained that should the King marry Mrs Simpson she would become Queen, an eventuality

The King on a visit to miners in South Wales. Touched by their plight, he offered both sympathy and support.

that the British people would probably not accept. In reply the King stated that he fully intended to marry Mrs Simpson as soon as she was free, and if the Government opposed the match then, he said, he was 'prepared to go.' Unable to comment for the moment on this 'most grievous news,' Baldwin left the King, who presently joined his mother and sister for dinner at Marlborough House. He told them of his love for Wallis Simpson and of his wishes regarding her. Queen Mary, he later recalled, 'for all her self-control . . . was obviously distressed . . . [yet] expressed the hope that I would make a wise decision for my future. . . .'

During the course of the following day the King advised his three brothers of his decision. He also spoke with Sir Samuel Hoare and Duff Cooper, with whom he was on friendly terms and who both were senior members of the Government. Hoare thought that Baldwin and the Cabinet were determined to oppose the marriage. This the King must accept, but he

discounted Cooper's suggestion that the whole question be put on one side until after the Coronation, since this would have meant being crowned with a lie on his lips.

For the next two days, 18th and 19th November, the King was out of town touring the depressed mining villages of the Rhondda and Monmouth valleys. Here he uttered the well-meaning comments that something must be done to help the unemployed in South Wales, emphasizing: 'You may be sure that all I can do for you I will.' Popular as this pledge may at first have been, newspaper headlines the following day echoing 'Something will be done,' it was made at a critical moment when the King, having already told Baldwin, Queen Mary and his three brothers of his plans, was in no position to extend such hope to desperate people. Lord Rothermere's *Daily Mail*, however, published a leader on 23rd November entitled 'The King Edward Touch', in which the Sovereign was praised for his compassion and his forthright manner, by contrast to the slowly grinding machinery, not to say apathy, of Whitehall. The story amounted to an attempt to start a campaign in support of the King against the Government. This brought forth a declaration from *The Times* that while the King's contribution should be applauded, 'it is a wholly mischievous suggestion . . . which would set his well-known sympathy with the distressed areas against the measures taken by the Government, and which by implication would drive a wedge between the Monarch and his Ministers.'

What Geoffrey Dawson of *The Times* probably did not realize was that Lord Rothermere, whose sympathy for the King and Mrs Simpson's cause was then circulating, had already launched his scheme through the agency of his son, Esmond Harmsworth, an occasional

guest at Fort Belvedere. As chairman of the Newspaper Proprietors' Association, the latter
had been co-operating with Lord Beaverbrook in restraining the Press in its reporting of the
divorce proceedings at Ipswich. While the King was absent in Wales, Harmsworth had
lunched with Mrs Simpson, telling her that he knew of His Majesty's wish to marry her and
moreover he appreciated the difficulties involved. Had the couple, he wondered, given
thought to the possibility of a morganatic marriage? In the event of such with the King, she
would be denied the dignities of her husband and her children the rights of succession.
Harmsworth surmised that such a course would remove the most contentious aspect of their
union and thus avert the crisis.

Beguiled, Mrs Simpson conveyed the morganatic proposal to the King, who at first was
skeptical. In a move symptomatic of his increasingly agitated mental condition, Edward VIII
then considered the matter before sending for Harmsworth, giving him his permission to
raise the question with the Prime Minister. He also consulted Walter Monckton on the legal
precedents. Monckton, like Beaverbrook when he heard of the idea, advised strongly against
such a plan as undesirable; the obstacles in Parliament alone were sufficient to render it im-
practicable. Yet the King, despite his earlier protestations that he would 'go quietly,' now
pressed ahead because, in her ignorance of the real issue, it was what Mrs Simpson wanted.
Paradoxically, he did nothing to disabuse her. Blind to the trap before him, with but a single
aim in mind, that of spending the remainder of his life alongside his loved one, His Majesty
ignored every plea to reconsider.

Monday 25th November found Stanley Baldwin again in the presence of the King. Since
their last meeting the Prime Minister had been approached for his opinion, after which he
told Tom Jones, the Deputy Secretary to the Cabinet, that not only was he personally not in
favour of a morganatic alliance, he would also resign if required to put it to the Commons.
So, prior to his audience, Baldwin made sure of his ground by enlisting support against the
proposal from the leaders of both opposition parties. The King duly listened to and under-

stood the reasons from his Prime Minister's sentiments, but was nevertheless certain that he wished the proposition to be formally examined. Having explained what course he would therefore be obliged to take, Baldwin promised not only to bring the matter before the Cabinet but also to seek the advice of the Dominions' Prime Ministers.

Hurrying away, the Prime Minister at last knew that the King had provided him with the means to bring the situation to a head. The morganatic marriage proposal was discussed at an inner Cabinet meeting on 25th November and again before the whole Cabinet two days later. Baldwin wanted no immediate decision but would wait for his colleagues' views to be expressed when they gathered at Downing Street once more on 2nd December. Meanwhile telegrams were sent to the Dominions requesting a choice to be made between the King marrying Mrs Simpson (whereupon she would be recognized as Queen), a morganatic marriage, or that the King should abdicate in favour of his brother the Duke of York.

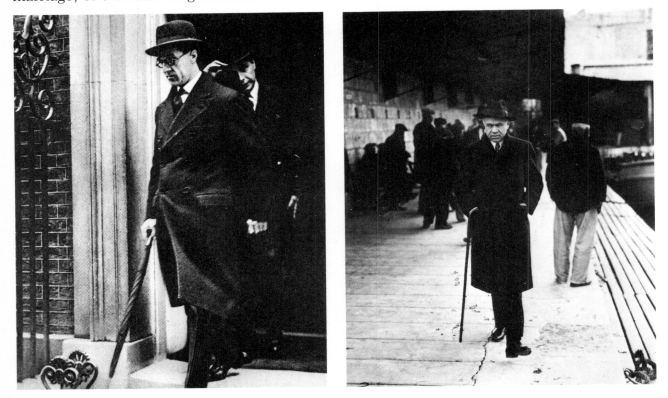

Walter Monckton, left, one of the King's most trusted advisers, leaving 10 Downing Street during the Abdication crisis. Right. Lord Beaverbrook.

Locked up in Cumberland Terrace with her aunt, strangers loitering on the pavement outside, Wallis Simpson 'began to feel like a hunted animal.' She received mysterious, unpleasant, even threatening letters, and when a rumour became current that her house would be blown up the King compelled her for safety to go with Mrs Merryman to the seclusion of the Fort. No sooner had they reached their destination than Mrs Simpson, in a state of nervous collapse, sensed that it was not at all the enchanted place it had been only a few short weeks before. She wrote in anguish on 30th November, three days after their arrival, to her friend 'Foxy' Gwynne: 'Everything is wrong and going more wrong. . . . I think I shall remove myself when I am well enough for a small trip and give it all time to die down.' To Sibyl Colefax on the same day she again intimated her intention of running away. But even if Mrs Simpson had been serious in her desire to vanish, coming events quickly assured that she did indeed quit the scene, although not as privately as she would have preferred.

Like a presaging storm in a tragedy, the Crystal Palace burned down on the night of 30th November. Its ignition, destroying an emotive monument to Victorian progress and tech-

Above left. The destruction by fire, on the night of 31st November 1936, of the Crystal Palace at Sydenham, a symbol of Victorian progress, seemed to symbolize the end of an era. Below. The British Press, for so long urged not to mention the matter of the King's relationship with Mrs Simpson, broke silence on the morning of 3rd December 1936. Above right. News of the constitutional crisis becoming known in the British Isles stimulated a short-lived wave of sympathy for the King.

nical ingenuity, the brainchild of Edward VIII's great-grandfather Prince Albert, loomed in the public imagination for days to come. The conflagration inflamed the clouds over all London, and by the time the smoke had cleared the following morning, Tuesday 1st December, photographs of its smouldering ruins appeared in every newspaper. Later that day Fleet Street began receiving news of another kind—on the face of it not very exciting—the text of an address made by the Bishop of Bradford, Dr A.W.F. Blunt, to his diocesan conference. Replying to a suggestion from the Bishop of Birmingham that the Coronation ceremony should be secularized, Dr Blunt had managed to infer that the King, 'for [he] is a man like any other,' was in need of divine guidance. This 'blow with a Blunt instrument,' as wags described the Bishop's performance, was what the British Press had been waiting for. After straining at their leashes for so long, newspaper editors now took the remark as a signal and broke silence on 3rd December.

Just as the *Daily Mirror* unveiled a large studio portrait of Mrs Simpson on its front page that morning, so the King was contemplating the outcome of his most recent audience with the Prime Minister. On the previous evening, that of 2nd December, Baldwin had confirmed what he already suspected, that the Cabinet and the Dominions were all but unanimous in their rejection of the morganatic marriage proposal. Having left the King with no choice but to abdicate in order to marry Mrs Simpson, Baldwin then begged him to think afresh, saying: 'All the peoples of your Empire, Sir, sympathise with you most deeply; but they all know—as you yourself must—that the throne is greater than the man.' To this and all similar arguments His Majesty made no comment, only repeating again and again as if spell-bound: 'Wallis is the most wonderful woman in the world.'

In Max Beaverbrook's colourful phrase, the King had indeed put his head on the Prime Minister's chopping block. Later that evening Edward returned to the Fort in a sombre mood to tell Mrs Simpson what lay in store for them both. She then telephoned Herman and Katherine Rogers at Lou Viei, their villa in Cannes, to ask for a safe haven. The next day, leaving

Villa Lou Viei, near Cannes, which Mrs Simpson used to escape while waiting for events to take their course.

her little dog Slipper behind, she embraced the King in parting. 'I don't know how it's all going to end,' she remembered him saying: 'It will be some time before we can be together again. You must wait. . . . I shall never give you up.' Lord Brownlow, the King's old friend and Lord-in-waiting, who had offered to accompany Mrs Simpson in her flight, now handed her into his car. Inspector Evans of Scotland Yard and Brownlow's chauffeur completed the party. Clouds dark and low, it steadily drizzled as they moved off towards Newhaven, the cross-Channel ferry and the start of a nightmare journey to Cannes (ills. 94 and 114).

Although between 4th and 7th December the King's friends, notably Beaverbrook, Rothermere and Winston Churchill, made strenuous efforts to reverse the situation, the fight was lost. Baldwin heard from Walter Monckton on Saturday afternoon, 5th December, of the King's final decision to abdicate. After the week-end and despite Lord Rothermere's last-minute appeals in the *Daily Mail* and *Evening News* for a pause, the country itself appeared to agree with Baldwin, his Cabinet and the Dominions. Members of Parliament, returning from

A HORNET'S NEST
POOR WINNIE-THE-POOH!

Winston Churchill, one of the few politicians who supported the King in the morganatic marriage proposal, was shouted down in the House of Commons on 7th December 1936. *Punch* celebrated the occasion with this unkind cartoon. Right. Wallis Simpson shortly before the abdication of King Edward VIII.

their constituencies, came into London with the overwhelming impression that the people were against the morganatic marriage proposal, were against the King and more especially were against Wallis Simpson. Even in South Wales, according to Frank Owen and R.J. Thomson in their book *His Was the Kingdom* (London, 1957), 'the King's popularity had gone. Cinema audiences saw in cold silence the films of his recent visit to the valleys where they had all cheered themselves hoarse. . . .' That any residual support for the King's marriage plans remaining in Parliament had also evaporated was apparent from Churchill's emphatic humiliation in the House of Commons. Afterwards *Punch* depicted him as a slightly baffled, sawdust-headed Winnie-the-Pooh tormented by hornets.

Edward VIII signed the Instrument of Abdication on 10th December 1936, and within twenty-four hours, announced by Sir John Reith as His Royal Highness Prince Edward, he delivered his memorable broadcast from a room in the Augusta Tower of Windsor Castle. 'At

INSTRUMENT OF ABDICATION

I, Edward the Eighth, of Great Britain, Ireland, and the British Dominions beyond the Seas, King, Emperor of India, do hereby declare My irrevocable determination to renounce the Throne for Myself and for My descendants, and My desire that effect should be given to this Instrument of Abdication immediately.

In token whereof I have hereunto set My hand this tenth day of December, nineteen hundred and thirty six, in the presence of the witnesses whose signatures are subscribed.

SIGNED AT
FORT BELVEDERE
IN THE PRESENCE
OF

long last I am able to say a few words of my own,' he began. After explaining that it had been constitutionally impossible for him to speak before, he now declared his allegiance to his brother, now King George VI. 'You all know the reasons,' he said, 'which have impelled me to renounce the throne. . . . But you must believe me when I tell you that I have found it impossible to carry the heavy burden of responsibility and to discharge my duties as King as *I* would wish to do without the help and support of the woman I love.' It was, he avowed, his decision alone: 'The other person most concerned has tried up to the last to persuade me to take a different course. I have made this, the most serious decision of my life, upon a single thought of what would in the end be the best for all.' The speech continued with graceful

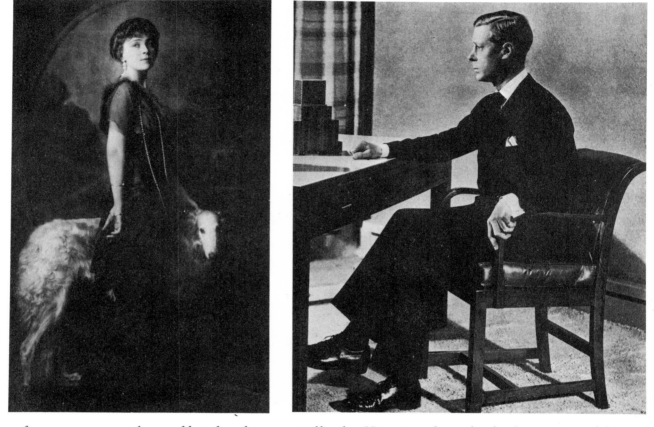

Baron Eugène de Rothschild, head of the Austrian branch of the renowned banking family, and his American born wife Kitty, left offered their home, the Schloss Enzesfeld outside Vienna, to the Duke of Windsor who was advised to remain separated from Mrs Simpson until her divorce decree became absolute. The Duke now began to realize the total isolation in which the Abdication had placed him, in spite of the fact that the couple communicated daily by letter and telephone. Right. Although this photograph is usually thought to represent the King delivering his Abdication speech, it was actually taken on a different occasion some months before.

references to members of his family, especially the King in whom he had every confidence, and to Stanley Baldwin and other Ministers of the Crown who had 'always treated me with full consideration.' Lastly he thanked the people of all classes throughout the Empire for their great kindness in the past and hoped that if in the future 'I can be found of service to His Majesty in a private station I shall not fail. . . . God bless you all. God Save the King.'

Mrs Simpson heard the broadcast on the radio at Lou Viei. 'I was lying on the sofa,' she wrote later, 'with my hands over my eyes, trying to hide my tears.' Immediately afterwards Prince Edward took an emotional leave of his mother, sister and three brothers before motoring with Walter Monckton down to Portsmouth. Arriving there late at night in an almost ebullient mood, he boarded the Royal Navy vessel *Fury*, with Slipper under one arm, to set sail for France early the next morning.

While Mrs Simpson and her friends were besieged at Lou Viei by a mob of journalists and news photographers, it was deemed expedient for fear of jeopardizing her divorce proceedings that she and the newly styled Duke of Windsor should avoid meeting until her decree became absolute (ill. 56). The Duke, who had been offered refuge by Baron Eugène de

Rothschild and his American wife Kitty, therefore travelled to Austria to stay at their Schloss Enzesfeld outside Vienna. According to witnesses, he began the long, lonely wait in the mood that had informed all his recent actions. Euphoric to the point of insanity, he had no regrets for what he had allowed to happen, 'the final catastrophe' as Ernest Simpson dramatically put it, happy in the knowledge that before long he would be reunited with the woman he loved. Despite the awful technical difficulties, the couple spoke to one another on the telephone as often as they could and corresponded frequently.

'Darling I love you. Come to me soon,' Mrs Simpson wrote on 1st January 1937. The Duke exclaimed in a letter, full of similar tender expressions, that crossed with hers: 'God! how I love you my Wallis my beloved sweetheart.' With the assistance of Van Cleef & Arpels' jewellers' skills, he translated these feelings into ruby and diamond 'feathers' for Christmas as well as a special gift for New Year (ill. 130). The latter, fervently inscribed 'No more like this Christmas 1936 Make come quickly,' takes up a recurrent theme in their billets-doux, that of their forthcoming union. His position altered and his official duties at an end, the Duke had little else to ponder but the future. He disliked the quiet and sedentary life at Schloss Enzesfeld, all the while yearning to be with Wallis Simpson. Moreover he wished to be rid of Kitty de Rothschild, who promised to quit the castle but found endless excuses for not doing so. 'All well here,' Godfrey Thomas wrote on 21st March in a letter to George Allen. 'Like those who have preceded me at Enzesfeld, I haven't for many years known my

While the Duke sought refuge near Vienna, Mrs Simpson had been staying with Mr and Mrs Herman Rogers at their villa in Cannes since 6th December 1936. Five days before the Abdication, in preparation for her marriage to the Duke of Windsor, she left on 9th March 1937 for the Château de Candé near Tours (left), lent to the couple by the wealthy industrialist, Charles Bedaux. Right. Gathered at the Villa Lou Viei at Cannes on 10th December 1936, left to right, are Lord Brownlow, Katherine Rogers, Wallis Simpson and Herman Rogers.

host in such good form . . . . But it is tragic to see the petty activities to which he has recourse, just to fill in the time.' 'Still,' he continued, 'whether it is counting the wine in the cellar, superintending the plucking [sic] of his dog, or examining the house books, it keeps him going till it's the hour for his next telephone connection. . . .'

Thomas also informed Allen that His Royal Highness was due to leave Enzesfeld at the end of the month for the Landhaus Appesbach not far from Salzburg. In preparation for this move, the Duke decided to send Slipper to Mrs Simpson at the Château de Candé near Tours, where she had been staying since early March. The dog arrived within a few days on 24th March, but to the couple's dismay and distress it was accidentally killed only two weeks later (ill. 145). To Slipper's mistress it seemed like an omen. Just as Herman Rogers, also at Candé with his wife, performed the burial, first wrapping the pathetic little body in a rug, so Mrs

Left. The future Duchess of Windsor, photographed by Cecil Beaton at the Château de Candé, just prior to the wedding. Right. The Duke and Duchess of Windsor with 'Fruity' Metcalfe, the Duke's best man.

Simpson wrote to a friend with more bad tidings. News had reached her that there would be a delay in the divorce proceedings, a small legal matter but one that would keep the Duke from her even longer. The waiting did not last however, for on 3rd May George Allen telephoned from London to say that the decree had been made absolute. Mrs Simpson then called the Duke, who made instant plans to join her, arriving at Candé at lunchtime the next day (ill. 114).

The Château de Candé, although at heart a sixteenth-century mansion, had been enlarged and romanticized in modern times and embellished with quaint gothic doorways and windows. Situated in the beautiful Indre and Loire region of France, it has a commanding view of the surrounding verdant countryside dotted with poplars and rustling willows. It was here 'in the shade of sunlit trees, where the thick grass was covered by daisies,' that Cecil Beaton, working for *Vogue* in the Spring of 1937, took some of his happiest photographs of Wallis Simpson. The château was then owned by the millionaire Charles Bedaux and his wife Fern, acquaintances of Mr and Mrs Rogers, who at the time of the Abdication had suggested the house to Mrs Simpson as a refuge from the Press. The offer had been declined at first, but then she and the Duke selected it, having first asked his brother the King, as the most suitable location for their wedding, the date of which was finally set for 3rd June (ills. 22, 92 [1] and 106).

For the Duchess the moment of her marriage 'was a supremely happy one' as she looked on that warm and sunny day from her husband to the small gathering of friends and to her Aunt Bessie, who had travelled so far to be present. Lady Alexandra and 'Fruity' Metcalfe were also there, he acting as the bridegroom's best man, holding a prayer book given by Queen Mary to her eldest son on his tenth birthday. The Rev. R.A. Jardine, a rather shady vicar from Darlington, had come out to Candé against the wishes of his Bishop to conduct the ceremony. Afterwards the newly married couple left on their honeymoon for the Austrian Alps, where they had taken the Castle Wasserleonburg for the summer.

The Duke and Duchess of Windsor at the Château de Candé on their wedding day, opposite. Photographed by Cecil Beaton, and right at La Croë, their villa at Cap d'Antibes, at the time of their first wedding anniversary, June 1938.

Optimistic for their eventual permanent return to England, the Duke and Duchess of Windsor were at first undecided upon their next move. In fact, the problem of where they should live proved to be a continuing one, partly because he preferred the country and she the town. As an ex-King, the Duke furthermore had very confused ideas about how he might best serve his country. For the moment, therefore, after leaving Wasserleonburg, the couple passed the winter of 1937/38 between a Paris hotel, the Meurice, and the Château de la Maye, a rented house at Versailles. In the spring they took a lease of the villa La Croë at Cap d'Antibes, where they appear to have spent their first anniversary (ill. 139). Later in 1938 they leased 24 Boulevard Suchet near the Bois de Boulogne in Paris into which they moved the following January (ill. 100). The Duchess, who was soon to pose for the portrait painter Gerald Leslie Brockhurst, lavished much attention on the furnishing of the two houses, spending many months with interior decorators and in hunting through antique shops for fittings. These she added to items shipped over from Frogmore, where the contents of the Duke's beloved Fort Belvedere and his apartments at York House had been stored. Every detail was supervised by the Duchess, of whom Frances Donaldson has remarked: 'Throughout her life the beauty and splendour of her houses was equalled only by the quality of her food.'

On 3rd September 1939 the Duke and Duchess were at La Croë with 'Fruity' Metcalfe. Communications between them and England were poor, and it was only through a telephone conversation between Metcalfe and Herman Rogers that they learnt of the latest political developments. On hearing the news, the Duke, dressed for swimming, walked to the edge of his pool and told his wife in a quiet voice, 'Great Britain has just declared war on Germany, and I am afraid in the end this may open the way for world Communism,' before diving into the water. He was naturally most anxious to return home to offer his services, but on terms which the British Establishment found difficult to accept. For one thing, the Duke and Duchess' well-intentioned but ill-advised unofficial visit to Germany, organized by Charles Bedaux in October 1937, ostensibly to inspect developments in mass housing, had been judged particularly unfortunate. After two weeks' cogitation, however, it was decided that His Royal Highness and the Duchess, accompanied by Major Metcalfe, should travel to England. Motoring secretly to Cherbourg, where they were met by Lord Louis Mountbatten, they then crossed the Channel in the destroyer H.M.S. *Kelly*. Disembarking on 12th September onto red carpets at Portsmouth in a blackout to strains of 'God Save the King' played by the Royal Marines, a piece of ceremony arranged by Winston Churchill, the party was whisked away by Walter Monckton and Lady Alexandra Metcalfe.

Meetings followed for the Duke with Leslie Hore-Belisha, Minister of War, before he and the Duchess left at the end of the month for Paris, once more with 'Fruity' Metcalfe. Here the Duke of Windsor was attached to the Army, but as the enemy approached the Duchess fled during the middle of May 1940 to a hotel at Biarritz. Leaving Metcalfe behind in Paris, the Duke followed on 28th of the month. The couple returned to La Croë in June but were almost immediately urged to quit France for a neutral country. Driven by the Duke's chauffeur George Ladbroke and accompanied by the Duchess' maid and others, they crossed the Spanish frontier to arrive at the Ritz Hotel in Madrid on 23rd June 1940 (ill. 140). After the bizarre events that followed, surely one of the strangest chapters in recent history, thoroughly investigated by Michael Bloch in his book *Operation Willi* (London, 1984), the Duke and Duchess sailed on the *Excalibur* from Lisbon on 1st August 1940 to Nassau (ill. 142), where His Royal Highness took up his appointment as Governor and Commander-in-Chief of the Bahama Islands.

Although the Duke and Duchess of Windsor looked forward on 1st January following to 'a happier New Year', neither 1941 nor their subsequent stay in the Bahamas was particularly happy. Writing to Mrs Merryman almost as soon as she had arrived, the Duchess complained of being 'almost knocked out by the heat.' Yet she and the Duke tried to make the best of it, only privately confessing their true feelings about 'this dump,' 'these sordid Nassau surroundings.' 'I hate this place more each day,' the Duchess told her Aunt Bessie on 16th September 1941, and two months later: 'We both hate it. . . .' They worked hard and did all that was expected of them, above all 'they gave not the slightest hint of being bored.' Besides

The Duke was as eager to serve his country in the Second World War as he had been during the First. After negociation with the British Government he accepted the post of Governor and Commander-in-Chief of Nassau in the Bahamas. Neither the Duke nor the Duchess liked the posting but they worked hard; he on his official duties, she on redecorating the crumbling Government House (left) and by assisting the Red Cross (overleaf) and other local institutions.

her many strenuous duties as the Governor's wife, the Duchess joined the Red Cross and became involved in other good works, including the setting up of an infant welfare service on the island. Life there might not have been entirely to their satisfaction; nevertheless, they always retained a fondness for the place, even a quiet pride for the work they had undertaken there. Indeed later, at the French mill-house, the Moulin de la Tuilerie that in the 1950's the Duke had converted for use as a country house, a room was set aside for books, maps and other souvenirs of the Bahamian sojourn.

Towards the end of 1944, the year in which the Duchess of Windsor underwent an operation for appendicitis (ill. 92 [3 and 7]), the Duke began to realize that he would serve no useful purpose by remaining in Nassau. He therefore applied to the British Government for another post, but when none suitable was offered he decided for the time being to retire from public life. On 16th March 1945, five months before the end of his term as Governor, the Duke tendered his resignation. Owing to the continuing war in the Pacific, he and the Duchess were prevented from returning to Europe and thus spent that summer in America. Finally on 15th September they sailed from New York aboard the S.S. *Argentina*, arriving on 22nd at the Boulevard Suchet. The Duchess' happiness at finding the place unscathed by war,

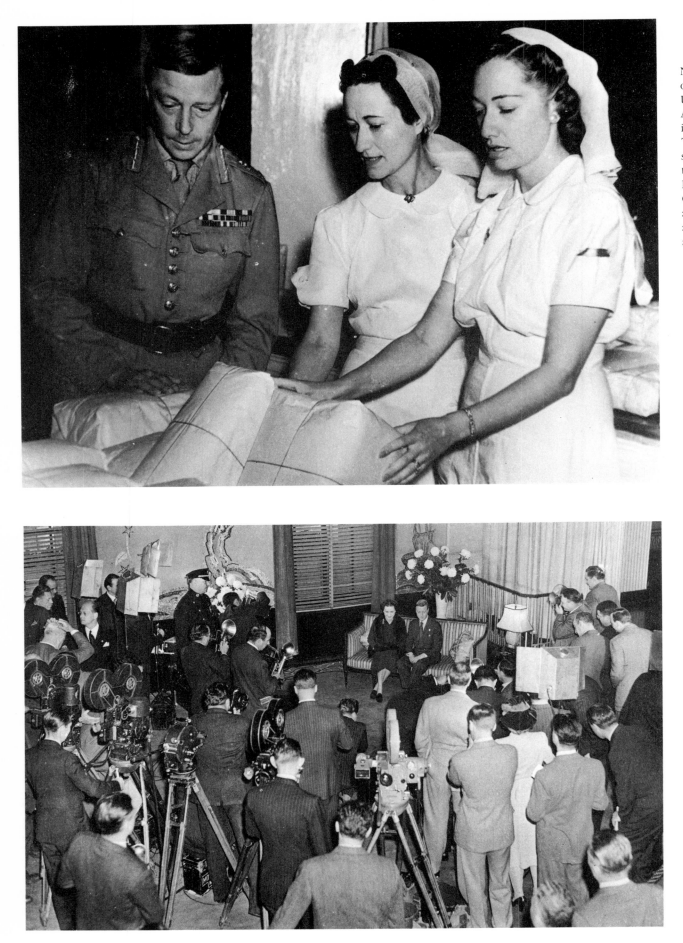

Ｆrom Nassau, the Windsors occasionally visited the United States of America although not in an official capacity. They are seen below shortly after the War at the Waldorf Astoria Hotel in New York City where an apartment was set aside for their many subsequent visits.

everything there 'looking really lovely . . . after five years away,' was broken by discovering that the lease had lapsed in their absence, and the house was sold. She sadly told her aunt: 'We have to move . . . to start packing December First. You can't imagine how I hate to leave and feel I shall go mad if we do not finally settle somewhere. . . .' Nevertheless, it was good to be back in Paris, especially for the Duchess, who assuaged her disappointment by costly visits to dressmakers and to Cartier, where she ordered an arresting gem-studded gold necklace (ill. 147).

Hunting again for somewhere to live, the couple stayed at the Ritz in Paris before repairing in December 1945 to another hotel in the South of France (ill. 96). Once redecorating had been completed in April, they returned to La Croë, their villa at Cap d'Antibes, remaining there until the autumn. Then, after a short trip to the Duke's ranch in Alberta, Canada, which he had purchased in 1919, they travelled to England, the first time the Duchess had been back since 1940. The Duke, however, had gone to London more than once since the end of the War to discuss with the King and Government the possibility of some sort of employment. Although Anthony Eden, when Prime Minister, considered offering him an ambassadorial post in 1955, the Duke was never again given the opportunity to serve his country.

Meanwhile in October 1946, having hoped that their return to Britain together might pass unnoticed, the Duke and Duchess of Windsor found their privacy suddenly shattered. They were guests of Lord Dudley at Ednam Lodge in Berkshire when the contents of the Duchess' jewel box were stolen. Dramatic accounts appeared in the Press of how the burglar

After the War, with no official role to play, the Duke and Duchess of Windsor, led a somewhat nomadic existence, lionized by society. To the delight of the international Press, they travelled constantly with mountains of luggage from Paris, to New York and Palm Beach. The Duke, remaining a leader of men's fashion, played golf, gardened and wrote his memoirs, while the Duchess enjoyed a reputation as one of the world's best-dressed women and finest hostesses.

had made away with so many valuable items that, scarcely able to carry them all, he had dropped some in his flight: gold cigarette cases on a windowsill, odd earrings scattered over a nearby golf course. Apart from these, none of the haul was ever seen again. Subsequent investigations by Scotland Yard revealed that the Duchess' loss was relatively modest because most of her collection had been left in France. But of the pieces which vanished she probably most regretted her newly acquired bird-of-paradise brooch, as stylish as the multi-coloured flamingo of 1940 (ill. 140). Created by Cartier from the stones of no less than sixteen existing jewels, it had been composed of one large cabochon sapphire together with a mass of other sapphires and diamonds arranged as a long sweep of tail feathers.

By November the Windsors had sailed the Atlantic to stay at the Waldorf-Astoria in New York, accompanied, so journalists never tired of telling their readers, with a vast pile of luggage. On this occasion, it was said, the Duchess had with her fifty different outfits from the best of Paris fashion houses. Afterwards, they went to Palm Beach for the season early in 1947 (ill. 47), then back to the Ritz in Paris in early June via New York and London, making the Channel crossing to France on their tenth wedding anniversary (ill. 166).

So began a pattern of travel that the Duke and Duchess were to repeat many times. He, often ill at ease with city life, sometimes frankly bored, would always indulge his wife, an inveterate party-goer, when they themselves were not entertaining. Although the Windsors were never without company, a large group of their friends and acquaintances leading the same kind of wealthy, semi-nomadic existence, the Duke was still hankering after some occupation. Then in the summer of 1947 at La Croë he began work on his autobiography, to be published three and a half years later under the title *A King's Story*. Having had previous discussions about the project with Charles J. V. Murphy, an editor with the American *Life* magazine, the Duke persuaded him to assist, promising that the results of their work could be condensed for serialization. Imagining that it might take a year at most to compile, Murphy was optimistic; the project was delayed, however, 'thanks in part,' so he wrote in 1979,

'. . . to the Windsors' sudden decision in early 1949 to give up both the Ritz apartment and La Croë.'

But before that, in February 1948, the year in which the first of the Duchess' great cats insinuated itself into her collection of jewels (ill. 187), the Windsors stayed as usual in Palm Beach (ill. 142). Here, it seems, she created a sensation by wearing the pair of 'priceless' yellow pear-shaped diamonds of 'exquisite brilliancy and lustre,' which she subsequently purchased from Harry Winston of New York, proof of her fixation for really big gemstones (ill. 203). A fire at the Duke's Alberta ranch in March destroyed a number of purebred Shorthorn cattle valued at $20,000, but, unperturbed, the couple completed plans for renting a large house next to a golf course for the summer in Locust Valley.

The wrench in leaving Cap d'Antibes in 1949 was considerable, and the Duchess always regretted the decision. It had been taken, she said, because 'the Côte d'Azur no longer seemed the same . . . a new type of tourist was swarming in. . . .' The Duke furthermore failed to enjoy his favourite recreation there because in summer the grass on the few nearby golf courses was always brown and burnt for lack of water. Almost as if to remind herself of the deep blue Mediterranean sky, the Duchess that year added sapphires to her collection, including a great cabochon upon which lingered a fire-eyed panther (ills. 116, 117, 151 and 179). But despite the disappointment in quitting the French Riviera, she was able to congratulate herself in the spring by finally finding a house in Paris. This was 85 Rue de la Faisanderie near the Étoile, which with her customary energy and perception for detail, the Duchess set about to transform into a proud residence. Before the summer the Windsors went over to New York, where they bought the celebrated McLean diamond (ill. 214), but then the Duke had to return to Europe alone to see his mother, whose health was beginning to fail.

The early 1950's, years that on the whole the Duke found rather trying, were enlivened only by the success of his memoirs. *A King's Story* was finally published in 1951 and received generally good critical reviews. To some, however, including surviving members of his staff who remembered the Abdication with great clarity, it caused concern, even anger at the way facts had been skillfully manipulated. In the words of Noel Annan writing in the *New Statesman*, the Duke had cleverly managed 'to lift the veil while concealing everything of real value.' Yet the book, which sold hundreds of thousands of copies, provided a healthy income and was even translated into a film that made striking use of old newsreels (ill. 196). George VI died in 1952, and the following year saw the death of Queen Mary a few months short of her eight-sixth birthday.

During 1953 the Duke and Duchess of Windsor moved from the Rue de la Faisanderie to a splendid mansion, at 4 Route du Champ d'Entraînement on the edge of the Bois de Boulogne. This large house, which had been occupied after the War by General Charles de Gaulle, actually belonged to the City of Paris, whose administrators were delighted to offer it on a long lease to the couple at a nominal annual rent. Set in a two-acre garden, tall green hedges shielding it from the street, it was here that the Duchess created her most beautiful interiors, luxurious settings for her celebrated evening parties at which no more than twelve or sixteen would sit down to be waited upon royally by liveried footmen in powdered wigs. But, as the Duchess admitted in her own autobiography, *The Heart Has Its Reasons*, written also with the assistance of Charles J. V. Murphy and published in 1956, the acquisition of this lovely house did not satisfy the Duke's craving for the country.

By a happy chance a year before they moved to the Bois de Boulogne, the Duchess happened to find an old mill-house with its various barns and subsidiary buildings near the village of Gif-sur-Yvette, forty-five minutes' drive from Paris. Called the Moulin de la Tuilerie, it belonged to a friend, the French painter Adrien Drian, who had carried out only partial renovations. Now, having first obtained a lease on the property and then buying it outright, the Windsors enthusiastically set about its conversion. On their first visit, while the Duchess contemplated the problems involved in remodelling such an old range of buildings, some of which had walls two feet thick, the Duke 'was already joyfully marking out with his eye where the herbaceous borders and the planting of perennials would go.' As with her other houses, the Duchess spent a fortune in its decoration and furnishing, and by the time James Pope-Hennessy visited them there in 1958 in his search for material for his life of Queen Mary, the task was complete. He was impressed by their luxurious life-style, observing of a much-loved member of the Royal Family living in a London palace that she was 'leading a lodging-house existence' by comparison.

As the Windsors celebrated their twentieth wedding anniversary in 1957 (ill. 90), so the Duchess' vivacity and sparkling manner at their favourite international gatherings seemed only slightly diminished with the passing years. Interest in fashion and jewellery was still of importance to her, even to the extent of having the emerald from her engagement ring re-set (ill. 120). Then in the mid-1960's, as if to re-affirm her unflagging sense of fun, the Duchess acquired, from David Webb in New York, gold-studded shell earrings and an amusing frog bangle with a matching pair of earrings (ills. 174, 176, 177 and 178). Like all the other animals and birds in her jewellery menagerie, these were echoes of her 1936 trousseau, which included a day dress in black crepe strewn with white turtles, another outfit in pale blue scat-

The Moulin de la Tuilerie at Gif-sur-Yvette, less than an hour's drive from Paris, was the scene of many week-end parties. Its interiors were reminiscent of an English country house and the attention given to guests' comfort became legendary. The Duke was particularly happy here, spending much of his time in the garden.

After the War, the City of Paris offered the Duke and Duchess of Windsor a magnificent house, set in the Bois de Boulogne near the Longchamp race-track. Set in a two-acre garden, tall green hedges shielding it from the street, it was here that the Duchess created her most beautiful interiors. The house contained many antiques and portraits of the Duchess by the world's greatest photographers.

77

Above. In May 1972, on an official visit to France, Her Majesty the Queen and Their Royal Highnesses Prince Philip and the Prince of Wales called upon the Duke and Duchess of Windsor at their house in the Route du Champ d'Entraînement. Although the Duke was gravely ill, he chatted with Her Majesty for nearly an hour; he died a few days later on 28th May. Below. The Duke of Windsor's body was brought with full honours to England on 31st May 1972 to be interred at the royal burial ground at Frogmore after a service at St. George's Chapel, Windsor Castle. The Duchess, meanwhile, stayed briefly at Buckingham Palace where she was photographed opposite on 2nd June, the day before her thirty-fifth wedding anniversary.

tered with a flight of yellow butterflies and an evening dress printed with an enormous red lobster.

Yet from now on the couple were often worried by problems concerning their health. In 1965 the Duke underwent an eye operation in the London Clinic, while also complaining of other complications. By May 1972, when they received a visit at the Route du Champ d'Entraînement from Her Majesty the Queen and Their Royal Highnesses Prince Philip and the Prince of Wales, the Duke had had several further operations. Very seriously ill with cancer of the throat, he died a few days later on 28th May.

The Duke of Windsor's body was removed on 31st May, with full honours, to England. On Saturday evening 3rd June, his widow, who had sent a spray of flowers that covered the entire length of the coffin, was driven down to St George's Chapel, Windsor, to witness the lying-in-state. By coincidence it was her thirty-fifth wedding anniversary. An estimated fifty-seven thousand people came to pay their last respects during the two subsequent days. The funeral on 5th June was followed, according to the Duke's wishes, by an interment at the royal burial ground at Frogmore, which, by arrangements made at the time, was also to be the last resting place of his wife. Afterwards the Duchess, who had been a guest for three days at Buckingham Palace, was taken to Heathrow Airport, where, 'a thin, tiny veiled figure all in black,' she boarded a plane for Paris.

The loneliness of widowhood was only partially mitigated by the attentions of friends and advisers. Inevitably with the approach of old age, the Duchess of Windsor's activities became more restricted, and in 1975 when seventy-nine she made her last trip to America not long after recovering from a broken hip. Still intensely concerned about her personal appearance, yet fragile and confused, she latterly confined herself to the house in the Bois de Boulogne, where she died on 24th April 1986.

The Duchess of Windsor, right, photographed on 11th July 1973 flanked by Lord Mountbatten and H.R.H. The Duke of Kent standing by the grave of her late husband. After a long period of declining health, she died in Paris on 24th April 1986. She is buried next to the Duke of Windsor at Frogmore.

Bibliography

Birmingham, Stephen, *Duchess*, Futura Publications, London, 1986.

Bloch, Michael, *The Duke of Windsor's War*, Weidenfeld & Nicolson, London, 1982.

_____, ed., *Intimate Correspondence of the Duke and Duchess of Windsor*, Weidenfeld & Nicolson, London, 1986.

Bryan, J., III, and Charles J. V. Murphy, *The Windsor Story*, Granada Publishing, London, 1979.

Donaldson, Frances, *Edward VIII*, Weidenfeld & Nicolson, London, 1974, new edition, 1986.

Inglis, Brian, *Abdication*, Hodder & Stoughton, London, 1966.

Windsor, the Duchess of, *The Heart Has Its Reasons*, Michàel Joseph, London, 1956.

Windsor, the Duke of, *A King's Story*, Cassel & Co Ltd, London, 1951.

Quotations from *The Royal Jewels*, by Suzy Menkes (London, 1986), are by kind permission of Grafton Books.

Quotations from *Diaries and Letters of Marie Belloc Lowndes*, edited by Suzan Lowndes (London, 1971), are by kind permission of Chatto & Windus.

Quotations from the *Wandering Years : Diaries 1922-1939*, by Cecil Beaton (London, 1961), are by kind permission of Weidenfeld & Nicolson.

Quotations from *Harold Nicolson : Diaries and Letters 1930-1939*, edited by Nigel Nicolson (London, 1966), are by kind permission of Collins.

Quotations from *Chips : The Diaries of Sir Henry Channon*, edited by Robert Rhodes James (London, 1967), are by kind permission of Weidenfeld & Nicolson.

Quotations from *The Heart Has Its Reasons*, by the Duchess of Windsor (London, 1956), is by kind permission of the Duchess of Windsor's Estate and Michael Joseph Ltd.

Quotations from *A King's Story*, by the Duke of Windsor (London, 1951), is by kind permission of the Duchess of Windsor's Estate.

Quotations from *Wallis & Edward, Letters 1931-1937* ; *The Intimate Correspondence of the Duke and Duchess of Windsor*, edited by Michael Bloch (London, 1986), is by kind permission of the Duchess of Windsor's Estate and Michael Bloch.

Desk Seals, Objets de vertu and Silver

Two hundred and more years ago, fashionable London flocked for its shopping not to Mayfair or Knightsbridge, but to the area around St Paul's Cathedral and down nearby Ludgate Hill to Fleet Street. Shops and warehouses specializing in all the variety of merchandise imported from India and the Far East lay side by side with those whose ingeniously crafted jewellery, silver and costly objects of vertu were known in every part of the globe.

One such firm, the Crown Jewellers before the continuing business of R. & S. Garrard & Co were appointed in 1842, was that of Rundell, Bridge & Rundell (ills. 58 and 60), whose premises were once said to exceed 'all others in the British Empire, if not in the whole world, for the value of its contents.' In the 1830's their bowing shopman may have induced the Countess of Blessington to succumb to a whole suite of jewellery to complement her other purchases, but he could just as well have steered her towards a case of watches or antique cameos or even an entire silver-gilt dinner service, so extensive were the activities of Rundell, Bridge & Rundell.

The partners in this remarkable business set a standard in the goldsmiths' trade to which all similar firms aspired, and throughout the nineteenth century London boasted a number of such concerns. All would have had a stock of desk seals that, whether in the form of finger rings, pendant fobs or, as in the present collection, ornamental hand-held instruments, became as necessary to the leisured classes as inkwells and pens.

Each seal had a matrix of hardstone but sometimes of metal carved in reverse with a coat of arms, crest, initials or some similar device mounted usually in gold, silver, silver gilt or gilt metal. Seals were used for securing letters and envelopes by impressing the matrix into a special type of heated wax dribbled into position. The modern type of sealing wax, made from compositions of shellac, rosin and turpentine, is thought to have been devised in France during the mid-seventeenth century. Subsequently, great improvements were made in its manufacture, until by the 1850's transparent waxes and others of many delicate hues were available besides those in traditional black and vermilion.

Those to whom the possession of silver brings visions of the hideous Podsnap plate in Dickens' *Our Mutual Friend*, where 'everything was made to look as heavy as it could, and to take up as much room as possible,' might turn to other, more delicate items in the goldsmith's shop. The early twentieth-century manufactory of James Samuel Bell and Louis Willmott, while not a famous one, worked in a range of expensive materials for the best retailers of their time (ill. 46). The firm was to supply the amusing *bibelots*, the miniatures, snuff boxes and innumerable other 'little *things*', the like of which visitors to the Duke and Duchess of Windsor at Le Moulin de la Tuilerie found scattered on tiny tables. Unhappily, in 1906 Messrs Bell and Willmott decided upon a dissolution of their partnership. Two years later Louis Willmott, who had carried on alone, vanished from home one day hoping to delay his creditors!

opposite, top left to bottom right: ills. 1, 2, 3, 4, 5, 6, 7, 8, 9 and 10.

1. A GOLD AND HARDSTONE DESK SEAL
probably English, late 19th Century

With tapering lapis lazuli handle, the pierced, cast and engraved mount composed of scrolls and other motifs, the swivel double-sided oval agate matrix engraved with the Royal Armorials and the cypher of Albert Edward, later King Edward VII, *height 8.5 cm.*

2. AN ENGLISH GILT METAL DESK SEAL
circa 1823

In the form of a bust of King George IV *stuck on the reverse: Pubd by T. Hamlet 16 August 1823*, the columnar stem with oak leaf and acorn base, the hardstone matrix engraved with the cypher of the Prince of Wales, *7.5 cm. high.*

Thomas Hamlet, the celebrated early 19th century London retail goldsmith and jeweller, is said to have been born in 1770 at Boughton, Cheshire, the natural son of Sir Francis Dashwood. At first he became an assistant of Clark of Exeter Change, Strand, who dealt in cutlery, bronzes, clocks, watches, jewellery and silver goods. He then set up in his own shop in St. Martin's Court, later moving to 1 & 2 Princes Street, on the corner of Sydneys Alley, Leicester Fields (later Square), where early in 1797 he is described as a goldsmith and toyman.

During the next thirty years Hamlet's business flourished; according to an account in *The Gentleman's Magazine* at the time of his death, he was at one time 'reported to be worth half a million sterling.' Although he continued the business at 1 & 2 Princes Street, he diversified his activities, taking an interest in pearl fisheries at Bussorah and by building The Royal Bazaar, British Diorama and Exhibition of Works of Art at 73 Oxford Street. This burnt down in 1829. After further speculations, Hamlet became bankrupt in 1841 and his shop was closed and the stock of plate, jewels and jewellery was sold. He died on 21st February, 1853.

3. A GOLD CYPHER AND LAPIS LAZULI DESK SEAL
perhaps French, circa 1905

With the cypher of Edward VII, in the form of a column encircled with a chased and cast frieze of animal heads, and garlands, surmounted with a bust of a Roman emperor, *height 8.6 cm.*

4. A GOLD AND CITRINE DESK SEAL
English, circa 1936

With faceted tapering honey-coloured hardstone handle, the substantial moulded and lobed mount with citrine matrix engraved with the cypher of His Majesty King Edward VIII, *height 6.6 cm.*

5. A GOLD FOB SEAL
English, circa 1825

The tapering oval mount pierced and struck with reeded section, the faceted citrine matrix engraved with the phrase *Needs must when the Devil drives',* above an appropriate vignette, pendant ring, *height 5.7 cm.*

6. A GOLD AND HARDSTONE DESK SEAL
English, circa 1885

The entwined wirework stem supporting a lapis lazuli ball finial, the oval agate matrix engraved with the initials M. V. in monogram, below a royal coronet, *height 4.5 cm.*

The monogram is that of Princess Victoria Mary [May] of Teck, who, together with her husband, George, Prince of Wales, succeeded to the throne upon the death of her father-in-law, Edward VII, on 6th May, 1910. Queen Mary's eldest son, Edward, Prince of Wales, was created Duke of Windsor in 1936. For Queen Mary's silver-gilt christening set, part of which had been the gift of George III to his fourth daughter, Princess Mary (1776-1857) upon her christening in 1776, see Sotheby's, London, 24th April, 1986.

7. A GOLD AND HARDSTONE DESK SEAL
probably English, late 19th Century

With faceted tapering chalcedony handle, the similar matrix engraved with the Prince of Wales' feathers and mounted in gold carved and cast with scrolls, gothic apertures and masks, *height 8.1 cm.*

8. A GOLD AND HARDSTONE DESK SEAL
probably English, circa 1800

With replacement fungus-shaped bloodstone handle, the pierced and engraved gold mount with faceted rock crystal matrix engraved with the cypher of the Prince of Wales, probably for the Prince Regent, later George IV, *height 8.7 cm.*

9. A GOLD AND HARDSTONE DESK SEAL
English, mid 19th Century

With large faceted tapering bloodstone handle, the moulded and lobed gold mount with bloodstone matrix engraved with the armorials of Prince Albert, *height 8.6 cm.*

10. A BLOODSTONE AND GOLD DESK SEAL
late 19th Century

The triform swivel matrix with hardstone faces, engraved respectively with the cyphers of Albert Edward, Prince of Wales, later King Edward VII, the Prince of Wales' Feathers, and the Badge of the Order of the Bath, *height 9.3 cm.*

opposite, top left to bottom right: ills. 11, 12, 13, 14 and 15.

11. AN 18 CARAT GOLD CIGARETTE CASE
by Cartier, London, 1934

Rectangular with engine-turned decoration, *the interior engraved: David 29–11–34. George, dimensions 7.6 cm. x 10.6 cm.; leather pochette, impressed: CARTIER.* Together with a smaller case of similar design.

A gift from Edward, Prince of Wales, to his brother George, Duke of Kent, upon the day of the latter's marriage to Princess Marina of Greece.

In his memoirs, the Duke of Windsor recalled of his brother that he was 'Nearly nine years younger than I, [and] was sharply different in outlook and temperament from the rest of us. Possessed of unusual charm of

manner and a quick sense of humour and talented in many directions, he had an undoubted flair for the arts. He played the piano, knew a good deal about music, and had a knowledgeable eye for antiques . . . His tragic death in an aeroplane accident in 1942 while on active service cut short, at thirty-nine, a promising career.' [*A King's Story*, pp. 239/240.]

12. A SILVER CIGARETTE CASE
J. W. Benson of London, Birmingham, 1904

Rectangular gilt interior, *engraved: From G.R.I.H.M.S. Renown, India, Oct. 26th 1921*, the reverse enamelled with the Royal Ensign, *115 gms., 8.5 cm. × 6.5 cm.*

A gift from his father, King George V, to Edward, Prince of Wales, who boarded H.M.S. *Renown*, at Portsmouth 26th October, 1921, in preparation for his long voyage to India and Japan. See ill. 91.

13. A SILVER AND ENAMEL CIGARETTE CASE
maker's mark B. C. German, early 20th century

Rectangular, the cover with an enamel of a capercailye sitting on a branch, the gilt interior engraved: *Für Er-*

innerung an den Ersten Auerhahn, 8. April, Schoenbuch, Wilhelm 8.3 cm. × 7.2 cm.

The inscription in translation reads 'In memory of your first Auerhahn, 8 April at Schoenbuch, Wilhelm'.

14. A SILVER VESTA CASE
indistinct maker's mark Birmingham, 1915

Rectangular, *engraved on one side: David from Harry*, and on the reverse: *June 23rd, 1917; 45 gms.; 5.3 × 4.5 cm.*

The 23rd June, 1917, was Edward, Prince of Wales' twenty-third birthday; this was a present from his brother Prince Henry, later Duke of Gloucester.

15. A SILVER CIGARETTE CASE
retailed by Alfred Clark of Bond Street, London, 1911

Rectangular with rounded sides, *the cover engraved: G.R.I. Oct. 11th 1912*, surmounted by a crown, *the gilt interior engraved: For David from his devoted father*, fitted with vesta compartment and fusee, *95 gms.; 9.5 cm. × 6.5 cm.*

A gift from his father, King George V, to Edward, Prince of Wales, probably upon the latter taking up residence at Magdalen, Oxford, in October, 1912. [*A King's Story*, p. 92].

opposite, top left to bottom right: ills. 16, 17, 18, 19, 20 and 21.

16. A SILVER CIGARETTE CASE
W. Hornby, London, 1909

Rectangular with reeded body, the thumbpiece gem-set, the interior gilt and *engraved: David from Mama, Xmas 1913*, fitted with vesta compartment and fusee aperture, *160 gms.; 9.3 cm. × 5.7 cm.*

A Christmas gift in 1913 to Edward, Prince of Wales, from his mother, Queen Mary.

17. A SILVER CIGARETTE CASE
retailed by Alfred Clark of Bond Street, London, 1925

Rectangular, with engine-turned decoration, applied with gold with the cypher of Edward, Prince of Wales,

the interior engraved: Xmas 1925, David from Bertie; 140 gms.; 8.8 cm. × 6.7 cm.

A Christmas gift in 1925 to Edward, Prince of Wales, from his brother Prince Albert, later to succeed him as George VI.

18. A SILVER CIGARETTE CASE
importers' mark L.C.B. & Co., Ltd., London, 1925

Rectangular, with basket weave decoration on cover and body, *the gilt interior engraved: Darling David from mama, God Bless you 1925., 125 gms.; 10.1 cm. × 8.5 cm.*

Edward, Prince of Wales, returned from a successful tour of the world on 16th October, 1925 [*A King's Story*, p. 421].

19. A SILVER CIGARETTE CASE
maker's mark overstruck by Alfred Clark of Bond Street, London, 1908

Rectangular, engraved with the cypher of Edward, Prince of Wales, gilt interior *engraved: For Dearest David from his devoted brother Bertie, June 23rd 1915; 90 gms., 8.3 cm. × 5.7 cm.*

Edward, Prince of Wales, celebrated his twenty-first birthday on 23rd June, 1915. This case was a gift from his brother Prince Albert, later to succeed him as George VI. See ill. 57.

20. A SILVER CIGARETTE CASE
by J. E. Caldwell & Co., U.S.A., circa 1940

Rectangular with reeded body, the lid engraved: *David*, the interior *engraved: From Wallis, Nassau 1941, 9.2 cm. × 7.8 cm.*

21. AN AUSTRIAN SILVER CIGARETTE CASE
maker's mark A.K.O. (?) retailed by Carl Weiss, Wien, circa 1930

Of rectangular form with reeded body the thumbpiece with the initials W. E. entwined, *the interior engraved: Vienna 20-2-35 W. E., further engraved: Wien 17-8-35., and: "alle guten Dinge sind drei"., 3 × 3/3 × 3/36 Wien., 145 gms.; 7.2cm. × 6.8 cm.*

The Prince of Wales, later Edward VIII, and Mrs Simpson visited Vienna together three times, the first from 18th to 20th February, 1935, the second from 16th to 20th August, 1935, and lastly immediately after the *Nahlin* cruise, from 8th to 13th September, 1936. (See ill. 97.) A postscript to a letter from the Duke of Windsor, addressed from the Schloss Enzesfeld, Austria, on 22nd March, 1937, to Mrs Simpson, relates to the inscription on this case: 'A boy's [the Duke of Windsor's] new address: Landhaus Appesbach, St Wolfgang am Wolfgangsee. Salzkammergut. Telefon: St Wolfgang No. 9. "Alle guten Dinge sind drei" 3 × 3! [All good things come in threes.] Also [enclosed are] some pictures of the Landhaus—not "Pension"! [*Letters*, p. 300.]

opposite, top center to bottom center: ills. 22, 23, 24, 25, 26, 27, 28, 29 and 30.

22. A TWO-COLOUR GOLD AND SILVER SNUFF BOX
early 19th century

Of rectangular outline, the hinged cover with reeded rim, chased and engraved with a frieze of acanthus leaves and panels representing coursing, fox-hunting and pheasant shooting, between palmettes, now centred with an engine-turned cartouche, *the interior engraved: To David, with best love & all good wishes, Alice, Harry, and dated 3-6-37, straight sides and rounded corners, the base engine-turned, width 9 cm.*

A gift from his brother and sister-in-law, the Duke and Duchess of Gloucester, to the Duke of Windsor upon his marriage on 3rd June, 1937, to Mrs Wallis Simpson.

23. AN 18 CARAT GOLD SNUFF BOX
Frederick Marson, Birmingham, 1864

Rectangular, with rounded sides, engine-turned and engraved with scrolls and flowers, *the inscription erased, length 8.4 cm.*

24. A RIMINGTON WILSON 18 CARAT GOLD PROPELLING PENCIL
retailed by Alfred Clark of Bond Street, London

The body engraved with the initials A. E. below a crown, and the Prince of Wales' feathers, and Nov. 9, 1898, the terminal with a bloodstone seal engraved with the initials A. E., the body of the pencil engraved: *The Rimington Wilson pencil, length 6 cm.*

The 9th November, 1898, was the fifty-seventh birthday of Albert Edward, Prince of Wales, the eldest son of Queen Victoria and Prince Albert who would reign as Edward VII (1901/10).

25. A GOLD BOX
Paris, 1764

Rectangular with hinged lid, engine-turned decoration, *marked on lid and body, makers' poinçon P. F., par-*

90

tially rubbed, charge and discharge marks for Jean-Jacques Prevost, width 6.2 cm.

26. A SILVER TOBACCO BOX
maker's mark E. T. with three pellets below, London, 1691

Of oval form, the cover engraved with armorials, reeded and rope twist border, straight sides, the base with similar border, later engraved with the initials *O. T. A. R. D. within a leafy cartouche, marked on cover and base*, 140 gms.; width 7.3 cm., length 9.7 cm.

27. A TORTOISE SHELL AND GOLD MOUNTED BOX
English, circa 1815

Rectangular, with incurving sides, the cover engine-turned, with reeded rim, centred with an oval blue enamel medallion with the Prince of Wales' feathers in rose diamonds in relief, and the motto *Ich Dien*, for George Augustus Frederick, Prince of Wales, later King George IV, width 8.6 cm.

28. A SILVER TOBACCO BOX
probably Ambrose Stevenson, London, 1705

Of oval form, the cover engraved with armorials, straight sides, moulded foot, *marked on body and cover,* 125 gms.; width 8 cm., length 9.8 cm.

29. AN 18 CARAT GOLD PENCIL-HOLDER
Alexander James Strachan, London, 1824

Of typical form, with aperture for a pencil, the body engine-turned, the seal mount acanthus and thistle chased, containing a bloodstone matrix engraved with the royal crest, *length 10 cm.*

30. A GOLD AND ENAMEL SNUFF BOX
Swiss, circa 1820

Oval, the sides and hinged lid decorated with engine-turned grounds within borders of pale blue enamel and foliate spray motifs, the lid further applied with a painted enamel plaque of Diana and an attendant seated below an urn, *width 8.2 cm.*

opposite, top left to bottom center: ills. 31, 32, 33, 34 and 35.

31. AN 18 CARAT GOLD REPLICA TRAIN TICKET
Mappin & Webb, circa 1919

Rectangular, engraved: *The Canadian Pacific Railway Company extends the courtesies of its lines throughout Canada to His Royal Highness the Prince of Wales K. G., nineteen hundred and nineteen,* and signed: *E. W. Beatty, President,* the left hand corner with a circular emblem of the company in relief, *dimensions 6.4cm. × 10.8 cm.*

Edward, Prince of Wales, left England at Portsmouth on board H.M.S. *Renown* on 5th August, 1919, bound for Canada. Disembarking at Quebec on 21st August, he made an extended journey of the dominion until 10th October. Thereafter, he spent the remainder of that month and most of November, 1919, in the United States before rejoining the *Renown*. The Prince returned to Portsmouth on 1st December. [A *King's Story*, pp. 417/8.]

32. A GOLD REPLICA TRAIN TICKET
Canadian, 1927

Rectangular, *engraved: The Canadian Pacific Railway Company begs to tender to His Royal Highness The Prince of Wales the Courtesies of the Railway on the occasion of his visit to Canada in the year 1927,* and signed: *E. W. Beatty, Chairman and President,* also engraved and enamelled with two medallions, one with the Prince of Wales' feathers and the motto *Ich Dien,* the other with the crest of the Canadian Pacific Railway, *dimensions 7.1 cm. × 11.1 cm.*

33. A BRASS NAME-PLATE
probably circa 1910

Rectangular, *stamped: Edward of Wales; dimensions 7.7 cm. × 2.6 cm.*

34. FOUR SILVER WHISTLES

One with indistinct maker's marks, London, 1897, the body *engraved: David;* the second, *Sterling silver, maker's*

THE CANADIAN PACIFIC RAILWAY COMPANY
extends the courtesies of its lines throughout Canada
TO
His Royal Highness The Prince of Wales, K.G.
nineteen hundred and nineteen

President

The Canadian Pacific Railway Company
begs to tender to
His Royal Highness
The Prince of Wales,
the courtesies of the Railway
on the occasion of his visit to Canada
in the year 1927

Chairman and President

EDWARD OF WALES

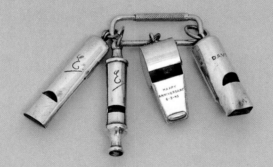

H.R.H. PRINCE EDWARD OF WALES.
R.N.

mark *C. E. A.*, engraved on the body with the initial E.; the third, *Sterling silver, maker's mark C. E. A.* engraved with the initial E., the fourth, *Sterling silver, numbered 744, engraved: Happy Anniversary 6-3-45.*

The date of 3rd June, 1945, on the last whistle seen here refers to the eighth wedding anniversary of the Duke and Duchess of Windsor.

35. A BRASS NAME-PLATE
circa 1911

Of shaped rectangular form, with apertures for screws, *engraved: H. R. H. Prince Edward of Wales R. N.*, dimensions 15 cm. × 8.3 cm.

Prince Edward served in H.M.S. *Hindustan* for three months in 1911.

opposite, top left to bottom center: ills. 36, 37, 38, 39, 40, 41 and 42.
36. A SET OF MAUNDY MONEY
1936

In a red leather case, with the profile of the King.

37. MEDALS: AN HEXAGONAL SILVER BROOCH-MOUNTED BADGE

Pierced with the monogram Eꝑ in modernistic style, Garter motto around, *rev. eng. Jan. 31st 1934-35', 42 mm.*; together with two white metal medals respectively, commemorating the Holy Alliance, 1854 and Albert Edward, Prince of Wales' Visit to Canada, 1860.

38. A PAIR OF 18 CARAT GOLD AND ENAMEL CUFFLINKS
by Simpson Benzie, Cowes, circa 1911

Each oval link enamelled in blue with an elephant above the motto *H.M.S. Hindustan, struck: Benzie, Cowes; enamel imperfect*; and a Medallion struck with the date: *June 22nd 1911*, the Holy Cross, and St George

and the Dragon, the reverse with the Fleet at anchor and the motto: *God be with you.* Almost immediately after his investiture at Caernarvon Castle, the seventeen year old Prince of Wales became junior midshipman on H.M.S. *Hindustan.* Joining at Cowes, Isle of Wight, he stayed aboard for three months from early August, 1911. (*A King's Story*, p. 80). The date of the coronation of King Geroge V and Queen Mary is that struck on the medallion. See also ills. 35 and 51.

39. A PAIR OF 18 CARAT GOLD, TINTED CRYSTAL INTAGLIO AND ENAMEL CUFFLINKS
English, circa 1915

Each circular link set with a crystal intaglio of the cyphers of King George V and Queen Mary within a blue enamel Garter motto.

40. A PAIR OF GOLD AND TINTED CRYSTAL INTAGLIO CUFFLINKS
English, circa 1915

Each with a pair of crystal intaglios with the monogram and crown of King George V.

41. A PAIR OF 15 CARAT GOLD AND PAINTED ENAMEL CUFFLINKS
English, circa 1905

Each with an oval terminal, one with a portrait of Queen Alexandra, the other with a portrait of King Edward VII, enamel slightly imperfect.

42. TWO CONFIRMATION MEDALLIONS
French, 1910

One in gold struck with the head of Christ by *F. Vernon, the reverse inscribed: Edward 24. Juin 1910*; the other in silver struck with Christ and a disciple, the reverse with the Holy Spirit and the Host, inscribed: *E. 24. June 1910.*

above
44. A PAIR OF GEORGE III
THREE-LIGHT SILVER-GILT CANDELABRA
AND A PAIR OF TABLE CANDLESTICKS
Matthew Boulton, Birmingham, 1808

The candlesticks with circular fluted bases, engraved with armorials, rising to ribbed flared stems, baluster sconces with fluted borders, the branches reeded and supporting gadroon bordered drip pans, *loaded, height of candelabra 56 cm.*

opposite, top left to bottom center: ills. 46, 45 and 47.

45. A WHITE ENAMEL PHOTOGRAPH FRAME
circa 1900

Circular, mounted with twenty semi-precious coloured stones, silver support, containing a photograph of Queen Mary, *engraved on reverse: George from Mary, May 6th 1935, diameter 6.5 cm. silver backing and support unmarked.*

A gift from Queen Mary to King George V upon the day of their Jubilee, 6th May, 1935.

46. A SILVER-MOUNTED
ALABASTER PHOTOGRAPH FRAME
Bell & Willmott, London, 1921

Hexagonal, applied with a gem-set trefoil motif and containing a tinted photograph of Queen Alexandra, *diameter 7.3 cm.*

47. A SILVER POCKET PHOTOGRAPH FRAME
maker's mark of W. F. Wright for Wright & Davis, London, circa 1898

Rectangular, *engraved: From Great Grandmama V.R.I. 24th May 1899,* the slide-action cover concealing an oval photograph of Queen Victoria seated, *7.3 cm. × 5.2 cm.*

A gift from Queen Victoria to her great-grandson, Prince Edward, the future King Edward VIII, on her eightieth birthday.

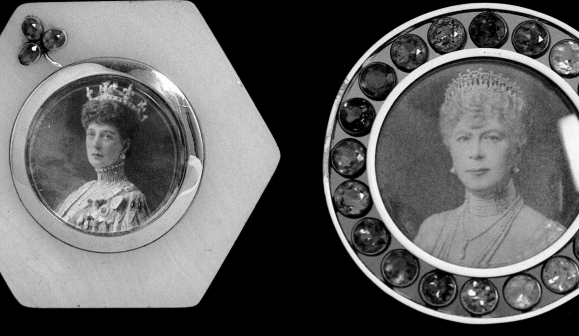

48. A GEORGE III SILVER-GILT RACE CUP AND COVER
Burwash & Sibley, London, 1810

Of campana form, on circular spreading foot with fluted frieze, the body engraved with an inscription on both sides, with a cast and chased frieze of vine leaves and grapes, reeded scroll handles rising from horses' heads and terminating in acanthus branches, the cover with ovolo rim rising to a cast acorn and oak leaf frieze, surmounted by a cast horse (badge of the Northamptonshire Yeomanry Cavalry), *marked on cover and body, 3060 gms.; height 40 cm.*

The inscriptions read: *Northamptonshire Yeomanry Cavalry, 24th August 1836* and *Pytchley Hunt Point-to-Point Steeplechase, Great Brington, 16th March 1921, Won by H.R.H. The Prince of Wales, "Rifle Brigade", Ridden by owner, Cup presented by the Master of the Pytchley Hounds.*

This cup was presented to the Prince of Wales, winner of the Pytchley Lightweight Point-to-Point, by Sir Charles Frederick.

The Northampton Races were held on 25th and 26th August, 1836. Amongst the races advertised was The Yeomanry Cup, each horse participating being the bona fide property of a Northamptonshire Yeoman and also to have been ridden by him five days at drill in the troop to which he belonged. The prize money of 50 guineas was raised by subscription by noblemen and gentlemen of the county.

(Compiled from information from a paper written by Reginald B. Loder Esq., which accompanies this lot. Mr Loder was a member of a well-known sporting family of whom several members were painters of horses.)

An illustrated article on the Duke and Duchess of Windsor's house, La Cröe at Cap d'Antibes, in American *Vogue* of 15th October, 1938, includes a photograph [p. 62] of 'The Dining Room—in yellow and white' which clearly shows this cup on a side table below a 'Portrait of the Duke in hunting pink.'

49. A GEORGE I SILVER-GILT CUP AND COVER
David Willaume, London, 1716

The domed cover with baluster finial engraved with a crest and motto and later engraved: *E.VIII R.*, the body with reeded rim and applied girdle, engraved on one side with armorials and on the other with the Royal Arms, scroll handles headed by acanthus leaves, on shaped spreading base, *marked on cover and body, 1565 gms., height 26 cm.*

50. A SET OF FOUR GEORGE III SILVER TABLE CANDLESTICKS

maker's mark indistinct, London, 1762

With square bases rising to fluted stems and Corinthian capital sconces, detachable gadrooned nozzles, the bases engraved, *loaded, height 30.5 cm.*

The inscription engraved on the foot of the base reads: *Presented to H.R.H. The Prince of Wales by the Merchant Taylors Company 12th July 1921.*

51. A SILVER TANKARD

maker's mark overstruck by Alfred Clark of Bond Street London, 1919, in Charles II style

The slightly domed lid with reeded rim centred with a silver gilt medallion of King Edward VII facing to dexter, *inscribed: Edward VII Crowned 9 August 1902*, the reverse with Queen Alexandra, facing to dexter, *inscribed: Alexandra, Queen Consort, 9. Aug. 1902*, with scroll thumbpiece and handle, the body engraved: *To dear David "Edward of Wales" from his loving Grand Parents Edward VII and Alexandra for his Confirmation 1910*; the base with reeded rim, *marked cover and base, 990 gms.; height 17.5 cm.*

Prince Edward, soon to become Prince of Wales, was confirmed on 24 June, 1910.

52. A CHARLES II SILVER TANKARD

maker's mark G. W. over a crescent and two pellets, London, 1677

With reeded rims, the flat-topped lid with bifurcated thumbpiece, the scrolled handle pricked with the initials *H.I.M.* and dated *1677*, the cover later engraved: *Drive contest between Houses of Lords and Commons. Twelve Birds, distance 25 yards*, above the crests of the House of Lords and the House of Commons, and below, *Won by F. S. Corrance Esq., against 15 competitors, Hurlingham Park, June 16th 1868*, the interior of the cover engraved with the Prince of Wales' feathers and the motto *Ich Dien*, the body engraved with the names of the competitors from both Houses with their scores, *marked on cover and body, repairs to handle and base, 740 gms.; height 17 cm.*

The names and scores of the competitors engraved on the body of the tankard are as follows:

HOUSE OF LORDS

H.R.H. The Prince of Wales	8
Lord Aveland	7
Earl of Aylesford	6
Marquis of Camden	8
Earl Cowper	7
Lord Huntingfield	9
Lord Suffield	8
Lord Willoughby de Broke	9
	62

HOUSE OF COMMONS

Lieut. Col. Hon. Annesley	11
Sir J. G. Hesketh	7
F. S. Corrance Esqr.	12
J. Milbank Esqr.	10
Viscount Holmesdale	11
J. Lamont Esqr.	10
Hon. A. Walsh	8
Hon. H. Wyndham	11
	80

opposite, top left to bottom center: ills. 53, 54 and 55.

53. A SILVER TOBACCO BOX
maker's mark J. H. S., London, 1935

Of oval form, the stepped cover engraved with the arms of Edward, Prince of Wales, the interior inscribed: *W. E. dec. 1935, marked on cover and base, 125 gms.; 7.5 cm. wide, 9.5 cm. long.*

The initials W E are those of Mrs Wallis Simpson and Edward, Prince of Wales (Wallis and Edward), in a form symbolizing their union in love. For comment on Christmas, 1935, which they spent apart, see ills. 92 and 124.

54. A SILVER TOBACCO BOX
makers mark F. R. T. & Co., retailed by Burfitt of Albemarle Street, London, 1935

Of oval form, the stepped cover engraved with the royal arms, the interior with the engraved inscription: *To remind His Majesty of many happy days at the Fort, and, incidentally, of Walter T. Prendergast. Easter 1936, Britannia standard, fully marked on base and cover, 150 gms.; 7.5 cm. wide, 9.6 cm. long.*

Walter T. Prendergast, a bachelor, born in 1898, was Second Secretary at the United States Embassy in London. A keen bridge player, he is often referred to in Mrs Simpson's letters to her aunt, Mrs Bessie Merryman, describing her life in the British capital. Prendergast was a frequent guest of Edward, Prince of Wales, at his retreat, Fort Belvedere at Sunningdale, staying there four times in 1935 and on five occasions in 1936 he was reposted by his government, a fact mentioned by the King in a letter to Mrs Simpson of 17th September: 'Good morning again my sweetheart as I've just talked to you. Your cold still sounds awful. Pooky demus! . . . Its [sic] sad about Walter Prendergast being transferred. I've asked him to come and see me this evening at 6.30 . . . !' [*Letters*, pp. 220/1, 319-322.]

55. A SILVER TOBACCO BOX
Crichton Brothers, London, 1935

The stepped cover engraved with the royal arms as borne by the Duke of Windsor, *Britannia standard, marked on cover and base, 145 gms.; 8 cm. wide, 9.5 cm. long.*

below
56. A PAIR OF SILVER SPIRIT LAMPS
William Hutton & Sons Ltd., Sheffield, 1926

Designed as Welsh dragons with detachable heads, on rectangular bases, *the bases engraved: from the officers of the Welsh Guards to Their Colonel and Cymru am Byth, 1700 gms.; of weighable silver; height 15.5 cm.*

57. AN ENGLISH SILVER-GILT CIGAR BOX
Carrington & Co., London, 1915

Rectangular, the cover with reeded rim, raised and engraved with the coat of arms of the Prince of Wales, the interior engraved: *TO HIS ROYAL HIGHNESS EDWARD PRINCE OF WALES. JUNE 23rd 1915 FROM THE MEMBERS OF THE KING AND QUEEN'S HOUSEHOLDS,* followed by a list of those members, *gilding rubbed on cover, 1,280 gms.; height 5.5 cm., length 26.7 cm.*

The names engraved on this cigar box read as follows:

MABELL AIRLIE	EVA DUGDALE	HARRY LEGGE
MARGARET AMPTHILL	FRANK DUGDALE	MARY MINTO
ANNALY	CHARLES FITZWILLIAM	FREDERICK PONSONBY
IDA BRADFORD	EMILY FORTESCUE	CONSTANCE
WALTER CAMPBELL	ISOBEL GATHORNE-	SHAFTESBURY
KATHARINE COKE	HARDY	SHAFTESBURY
CHARLES CUNNINGHAME-	BRYAN GODFREY-	STAMFORDHAM
GRAHAM	FAUSSETT	HENRY STONOR
CHARLES CUST	ALEXANDER HOOD	MARY TREFUSIS
BERTHA DAWKINS	PHILIPP HUNLOKE	HARRY VERNEY
DOUGLAS DAWSON	DEREK KEPPEL	EDWARD WALLINGTON
ETHEL DESBOROUGH	WILLIAM LAMPTON	CLIVE WIGRAM
	MARY LAMINGTON	

The 23rd June, 1915, which was Edward, Prince of Wales' twenty-first birthday, saw him on active service as a subaltern in the 1st Battalion Grenadier Guards in Northern France. At the time he was under the wing of the Corps Commander, Lieutenant-General Sir Charles Munro, living in a château near Bethune [*A King's Story,* pp. 113/114]. See ill. 19.

58. A SILVER-GILT SEAL BOX
maker's mark of Philip Rundell for Rundell, Bridge & Rundell, London, 1820

Of circular form, the hinged cover with a chased medallion of George IV, facing to dexter, wearing a laurel wreath and roman armour, inscribed: *Georgius IV Dei Gratia Britanniarum Rex,* surrounded by a ribbon tied laurel wreath and surmounted by a crown, the border chased with a frieze of oak leaves and acorns, the interior of the cover chased with an acorn wreath and inscribed: *Accessit XXIX 1 AN MDCCXX,* within a reeded border, further inscribed: *Presented by Her Royal Highness the Princess Augusta Sophia to Count Linsingen,* the interior with sponge, glass inkwell with silver-gilt cover and apertures for pens, straight sides and moulded base, *marked on body and cover, inkwell unmarked, 790 gms.; of weighable silver, 17.5 cm. diameter.*

59. A SILVER-GILT INKSTAND
Garrard & Co. Ltd., London, 1910

In the form of a royal seal box, the hinged cover with the royal arms, the border chased with oak leaves and acorns, the rim engraved: *Edward, Prince of Wales from his parents, June 23rd 1911,* the interior with glass ink bottle, separate pen holder and apertures for three pens, straight sides, moulded foot and reeded rim, *marked on body, cover and pen holder, maker's mark of Sebastian Garrard, 800 gms. of weighable silver; 18 cm. diameter.*

The 23rd June, 1911, was Edward, Prince of Wales' seventeenth birthday. Only the previous day his parents, King George V and Queen Mary, had been crowned at Westminster Abbey.

60. A SILVER-GILT SEAL BOX
Rundell, Bridge & Rundell, London, 1822

Of circular form, the hinged cover embossed with the royal arms within a border of oak leaves and acorns, the interior with sponge, cut-glass ink bottle and three apertures for pens, *maker's mark of Philip Rundell, the cover of the ink bottle with maker's mark of John Bridge, London, 1822; 650 gms. of weighable silver, 17.5 cm. diameter.*

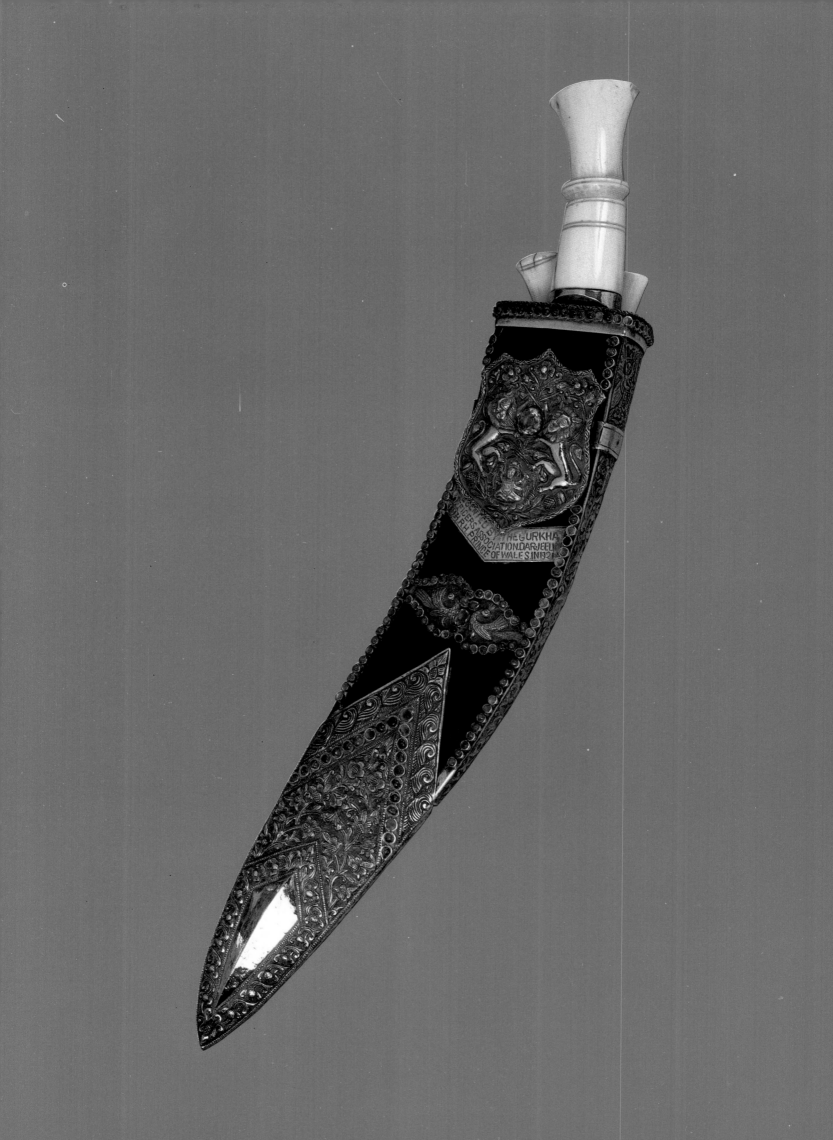

Swords, Knives Sporrans and Regimental Dress

George IV's timorous excursion of 1825 into Scotland was followed in due course by one of whole-hearted enjoyment on the part of his niece Queen Victoria and her husband Prince Albert. Thereafter all members of the Royal Family have loved the Highlands and the Scottish way of life, Edward VIII being no exception. As Prince of Wales, Edward had learned to 'blaw' on the bagpipes, a skill he practiced at the most unlikely times for the remainder of his life, occasionally, it has to be admitted, to the exquisite discomposure of his wife. He liked nothing better than to don Highland dress, as when he visited Balmoral with Mrs Simpson at the end of September 1936, just a few weeks before her divorce. The couple were photographed strolling together on the west terrace of Balmoral Castle, the King prominently wearing one of his silver-mounted sporrans (ill. 88).

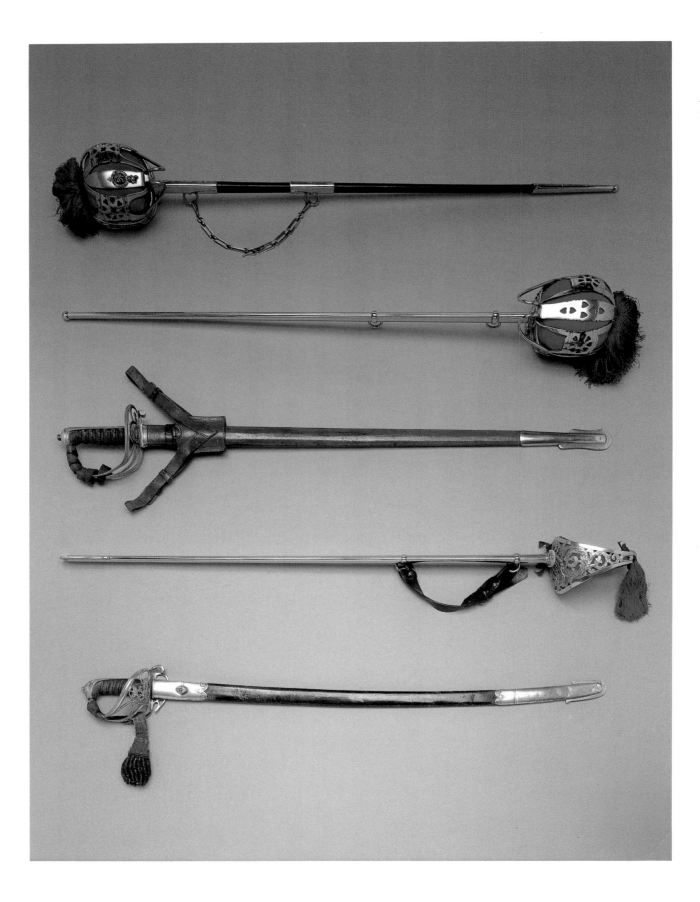

opposite part-title page
61. A PRESENTATION KUKRI MOUNTED WITH SILVER AND IVORY AND WITH GEM-SET SCABBARD
dated 1921

12 in. (30.5 cm.) typical blade inlaid with gold floral motif, ivory hilt, scabbard of horn plates sheathed in silver set with red, green and blue stones, embossed with a pair of gilt peafowl, the chape with gilt inserts, the mouthpiece with applied badge of two gilt lions rampant regardant supporting a blue stone over a figure of Shiva surrounded by Union sprays and a silver chevron inscribed: *PRESENTED BY THE GURKHA OFFICERS ASSOCIATION, DARJEELING TO H. R. H. PRINCE OF WALES 1921*, ivory handled skinning knife and steel, the back with detachable leather belt-frog, *42 cm. (16½ in.)*.

opposite, top to bottom: ills. 62, 63, 64, 65 and 66.

62. A SCOTTISH OFFICER'S BASKET-HILT BROADSWORD

32¾ in. (83.2 cm.), blade with single fullers, etched with panels of strapwork and inscribed on the outside *PRESENTED BY THE HIGHLAND SOCIETY OF LONDON JULY 1893* and on the inside etched with the monogram G within the Garter badge, the shoulder with double fullers etched with the Prince of Wales' crest and motto and the makers' name *Henry Wilkinson Pall Mall London*, the back stamped with the serial number *32178*, plated pattern hilt with applied silver Garter badge and monogram G, scarlet and buff lining and scarlet tassel, black leather scabbard with plated mounts decorated with strapwork, *102 cm. (40⅛ in.)*.

63. A SCOTTISH HIGHLAND REGIMENTAL OFFICER'S BASKET-HILT BROADSWORD
circa 1938

32⅜ in. (82.2 cm.) blade with single fullers, etched and engraved with thistles, the crowned Royal cypher *G VI R* and the regimental badge, motto *CUIDICH'N RIGH* and title of the *SEAFORTH HIGHLANDERS / ROSSSHIRE*

BUFFS, the shoulders with double fullers, inset proof mark *HW*, etched Royal arms and inscribed: *by appointment Wilkinson Sword Co. Ltd. London*, plated hilt, scarlet and buff lining and scarlet tassel, plated steel scabbard, *102 cm. (40⅛ in.)*.

64. A PATTERN 1854 SWORD FOR AN OFFICER OF GRENADIER GUARDS
dated 1914

32½ in. (82.5 cm.) blade, with single broad fullers, etched and engraved on the outside with the crowned Royal cypher *GVR* and twelve battle honours of the Regiment from *TANGIER 1680* to *NIVE* between bands of scrollwork, the shoulder etched with the Royal arms and inscribed: *by Warrant Henry Wilkinson Pall Mall London*, the back stamped with the number *44744*, the inside etched and engraved with the badge of the Regiment, a grenade and laurel wreath surmounted by a crown and a further eleven battle honours from *PENINSULA* to *MODDER RIVER* within scrolls and the Garter badge incorporating the Prince of Wales' crest surmounting the monogram *E* and inscribed *AUGUST 1914*, polished steel pattern hilt pierced with the badge of the Regiment, with remnants of leather knot, brown leather service scabbard with plated mounts, and frog with slings, *101.5 cm. (40 in.)*.

65. A SCOTTISH HIGHLAND REGIMENTAL FIELD OFFICER'S SWORD
circa 1920

34¼ in. slightly curved blade, with single fullers etched and engraved with thistles, the crowned Royal cypher *GVR*, and the regimental badge, motto *CUIDICH'N RIGH*, and title of the *SEAFORTH HIGHLANDERS/ROSS-SHIRE BUFFS*, the shoulders with inset proof mark *HW*, etched Royal arms and inscribed *by Warrant Henry Wilkinson Pall Mall London*, the back stamped with the serial number *59211*, plated bronze hilt pierced with honeysuckle scrolls (Royal Engineers Pattern) with scarlet and buff lining and scarlet tassel, plated steel scabbard, *104 cm. (40⅞ in.)*.

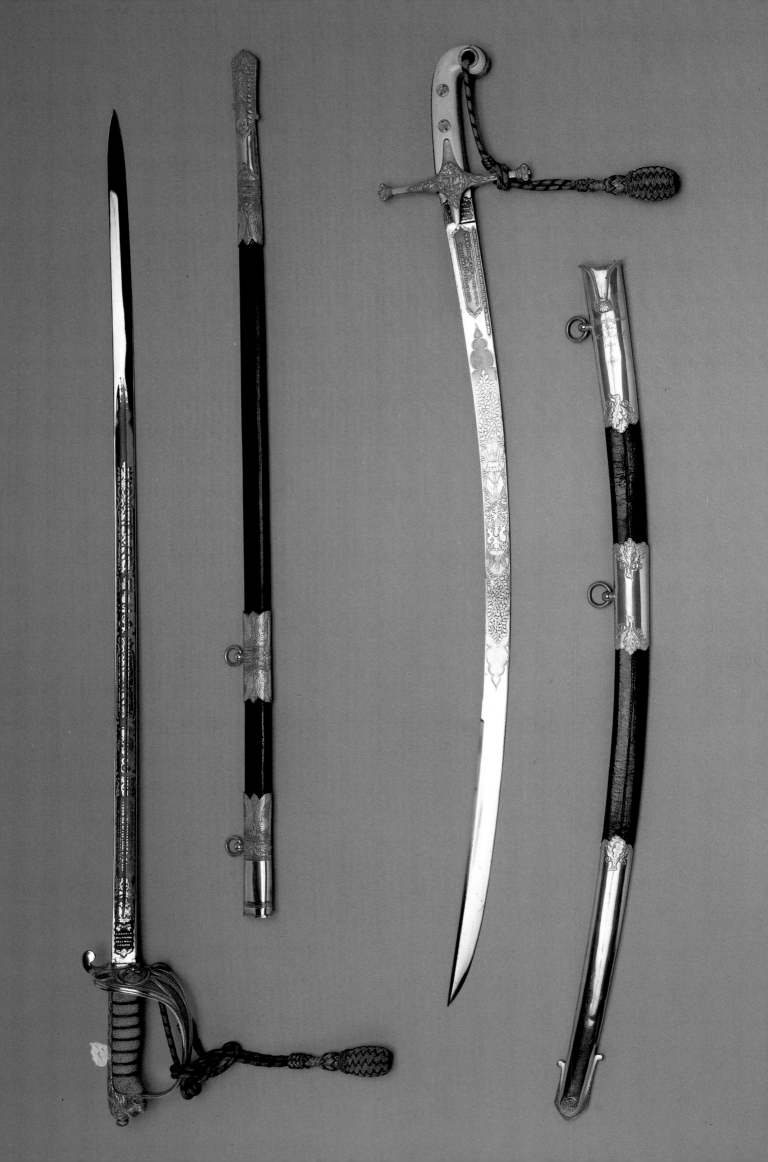

66. A PATTERN 1822 SWORD FOR AN OFFICER OF GRENADIER GUARDS
circa 1822

32⅜ in. (82.2 cm.) slightly curved pipe-backed blade with back edge at the point, etched and engraved on both sides at the forte with a crown surmounting a flaming grenade and the Royal cypher *GRIV within laurel wreaths, the shoulders inscribed: R. Johnston Sword Cutler No. 68 St. James's St London,* gilt bronze 'gothic' hilt with folding inner guard and cartouche pierced with the Royal cypher, gilt wire ribbon knot with crimson thread and bullion tassel embroidered with the Royal cypher and grenade badge, black leather scabbard with gilt mounts, the mouthpiece with frog-stud and inscribed: *R Johnston late Bland & Foster Sword Cutler & Belt Maker to his Majesty 68 St. James's London, 96.5 cm. (38 in.).*

opposite, left to right: ills. 67 and 68.

67. A ROYAL NAVAL OFFICER'S SWORD
dated 1913

31⅝ in. (80.3 cm.) slightly curved blade with single fullers, etched with panels of oak sprays within rope borders, Garter badges with Prince of Wales' crest surmounting the monogram E, the Royal arms and a fouled anchor, the outside inscribed *TO EDWARD PRINCE OF WALES LIEUTENANT R.N. FROM HIS AFFECTIONATE FATHER GEORGE, MARCH 1913,* the shoulders with inset proof mark *HW,* etched with the Royal arms and inscribed: *by Warrant Henry Wilkinson Pall Mall London,* the back with serial number: *44026,* solid pattern gilt hilt with folding inner guard, gilt wire knot and acorn with blue worm, black leather scabbard with gilt mounts, *96.5 cm. (38 in.).*

68. A ROYAL NAVAL PATTERN 1847 SWORD FOR FLAG OFFICERS IN FULL DRESS
dated 1856

29¾ in. (75.5 cm.) curved blade etched and engraved with the crowned Royal cypher VR, a fouled anchor, the Royal arms, crossed flags, a naval crown and sprays of oak, inscribed on the outside: *G. HENRY SEYMOUR TO HENRY KEPPEL 1856,* and on the inside: *LEFT BY KIND PERMISSION TO H.R.H. THE PRINCE OF WALES K.G. FROM ADMIRAL OF THE FLEET THE HON SIR HENRY KEPPEL, 1887,* shoulder etched with the makers name: *Henry Wilkinson Pall Mall London,* the back stamped with the serial number *7352,* pattern gilt mameluk hilt with ivory grips, gilt wire knot and acorn with blue worm, black leather scabbard with pattern gilt mounts, the mouthpiece inscribed *G. Henry Seymour to Henry Keppel 1856, 92 cm. (36 ¼ in.)*

below
69. A SCOTTISH REGIMENTAL SILVER-MOUNTED SKEAN-DHU OF THE HIGHLAND LIGHT INFANTRY
late 19th Century

3¼ in. (8.3 cm.), blade with fullers, scalloped at the back, typical hilt of blackened horn with embossed plated ferrule and pommel, the grip with applied silver badge of the Regiment, black leather sheath with embossed plated mounts, *21 cm. (8¼ in.).*

bottom
70. A SCOTTISH SILVER-MOUNTED DRESS SKEAN-DHU
late 19th Century

3¾ in. (9.5 cm.) blade with fullers, scalloped at the back, typical black wood hilt with chased ferrule and canted pommel, black leather sheath with chased mounts, the mouthpiece engraved with the Prince of Wales' badge and motto, *19 cm. (7¼ in.).*

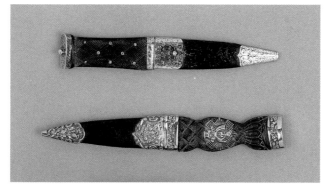

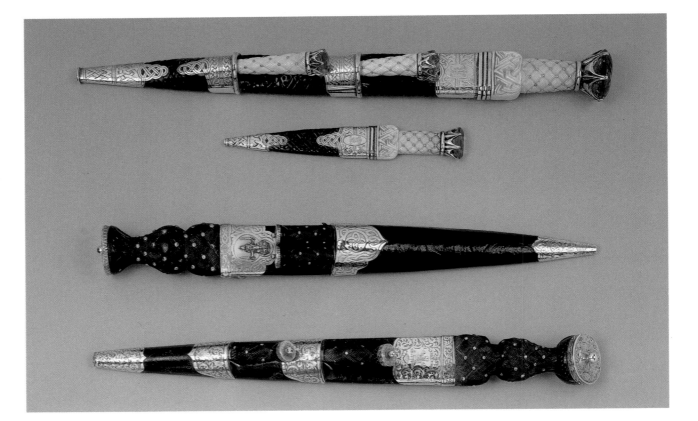

above, top to bottom: ills. 71, 72 and 73.

**71. A FINE CASED PRESENTATION
SCOTTISH DRESS DIRK AND SKEAN-DHU**
mounted with silver and ivory dated 1925

12⅛ in. (30.7 cm.), blade with fullers and scalloped back, ivory hilt carved with Celtic strapwork, gold studs at the crossings, citrine pommel in a silver mount, black tooled leather scabbard with chased nielloed mounts, the mouthpiece engraved with the Prince of Wales' crest and motto, by-knife and fork and skean-dhu *en suite*, all mounts with Edinburgh hall marks for 1923-24 and makers's mark *HI*, in a black morocco case lined with cream silk, the interior with maker's label: *Hamilton & Inches, 88 Princes Street Edinburgh*, the lid with applied silver plate inscribed: *THE ST. ANDREWS SOCIETY OF THE RIVER PLATE / PRESENTED TO / HIS ROYAL HIGHNESS THE PRINCE OF WALES K.G. / ON THE OCCASION OF THE / SCOTTISH CENTENARY FAIR / HELD IN PRINCE GEORGE'S HALL / BUENOS AIRES, SEPT. 1925.*

72. A SCOTTISH SILVER-MOUNTED DRESS DIRK
late 19th Century

11 in. (28 cm.) blade with fullers, scalloped at the back, typical black wood hilt with chased ferrule and flat pommel, black leather scabbard with chased mounts, the mouthpiece with applied crest of Scotland, by-knife and fork in paired mount, *43 cm. (16⅞ in.)*.

73. A SCOTTISH SILVER-MOUNTED DRESS DIRK
late 19th Century

10½ in. (26.7 cm.) blade scalloped at the back, typical black wood hilt with chased ferrule and canted pommel, black leather scabbard with chased mounts, the mouthpiece engraved with the Prince of Wales' badge and motto, by-knife and fork *en suite*, *43.8 cm. (17¼ in.)*.

$H$is Majesty the King, in *regimental uniform, during his visit to the Home Fleet at Portland.*

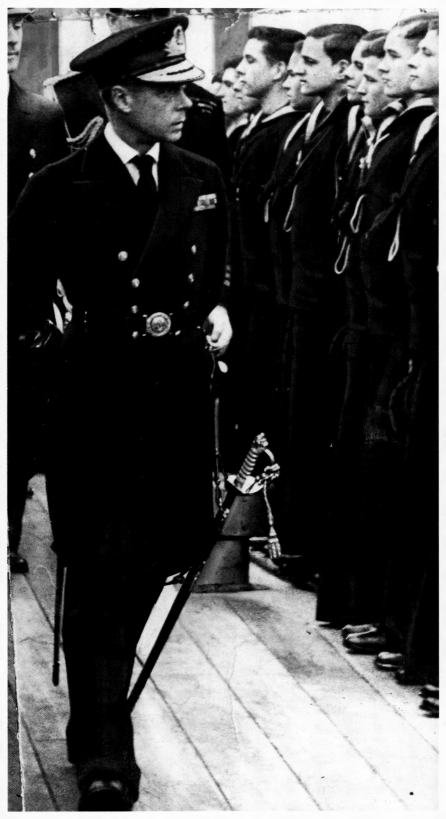

opposite, top left to bottom right: ills. 74, 75, 76, 77, 78, 79, 78, 80, 81 and 82.

74. A GILT AND SILVER SHOULDER-BELT PLATE

For an officer of the Seaforth Highlanders, *19th Century.*

75. A SILVER SHOULDER-BELT PLATE

Of the 72nd Regiment, the Duke of Albany's Own Highlanders, *19th Century.*

76. A SILVER SHOULDER-BELT PLATE

With the crest of Scotland and motto *IN DEFENCE,* the cusped corners decorated with strapwork, with a belt-clasp *en suite,* both with maker's mark *ht* and Edinburgh hall marks for 1934-35 and 1933-34.

77. BRASS BELT-CLASPS

Of the Grenadier, Scots and two Welsh Guards Coldstream and Irish Guards, *circa* 1920.

78. A GILT BRONZE AND SILVER BELT-CLASP

For an officer of the Grenadier Guards; and another of the Coldstream Guards *circa* 1920.

79. A BRASS BADGE OF THE GRENADIER GUARDS

Bearing the crowned Royal cypher *WIV,* accompanied by a brass plaque inscribed *W R IV CYPHER WORN BY A PRIVATE 1st Bn GREN:GDS: 1894.*

80. A CASE CONTAINING THREE SILVER PLAID BROOCHES

Two with the crest of Scotland and the motto: *NEMO ME IMPUNE LACESSIT,* one pierced with the badge of the *77th EAST MIDDLESEX REGIMENTS;* a crest of Scotland mounted as a brooch, a kilt pin and a plaid pin, the case lid bearing the hexagonal monogram of the Prince of Wales, *late 19th and 20th Century.*

81. FOUR CARDS

Mounted with buttons and insignia of the Grenadier, Coldstream, Scots and Irish Guards, a Major-General and the Leinster Regiment, *circa* 1920.

82. A CASE OF GILT LIVERY BUTTONS

Bearing the crest of the Prince of Wales and the monogram *HH,* six small and two large, by *Firmin & Sons Ltd, London, 20th Century.*

below
83. A SILVER-MOUNTED ALABASTER PHOTOGRAPH FRAME
unmarked, circa 1905

Oval, set with a cabochon turquoise and a gold bow, silver fittings, containing a photograph of H.R.H. the Prince of Wales, later Edward VIII, *height 8 cm.*

84. A LEATHER SILVER-MOUNTED SPORRAN

The mounts with indistinct marks, circa 1910, *dimensions 22 cm. × 17.5 cm.*

85. A SILVER-MOUNTED SPORRAN

The pouch of sealskin with six bullion tassels, mounts engraved with the crowned Royal cypher *GvR* and applied with the crest and motto of Scotland, the back inscribed in Gaelic and *signed MacShinidh (?) and with Edinburgh hall marks for 1911-12.*

86. A KID LEATHER SILVER-MOUNTED SPORRAN

The mounts engraved with scrolls, *dimensions 22 cm. × 18 cm.*

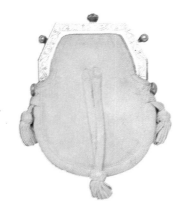

87. A KID LEATHER SILVER-MOUNTED SPORRAN
R. & H. Kirkwood of Edinburgh, Edinburgh, 1936

The mounts with stamped circular designs, *dimensions 22 cm. × 18 cm.*

88. A LEATHER SILVER-MOUNTED SPORRAN
Young & Tatton, Edinburgh, indistinct date letter, circa 1900

The mounts stamped with Celtic motifs, *dimensions 22 cm. × 17.5 cm.*

89. A SEALSKIN SILVER-MOUNTED SPORRAN

With silver tassels, *Edinburgh, 1911*, engraved with the cypher of King George V above cast armorials and the motto *In Defens*, the reverse engraved in Gaelic, *dimensions 22 cm. × 17 cm.*

The Prince of Wales in kilt at Balmoral with Mrs Simpson.

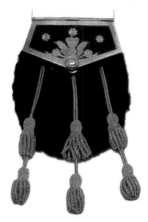

116

Jewels
of
The Duchess

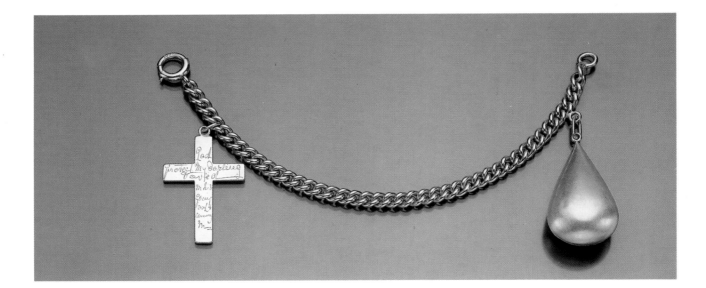

opposite part-title page
90. AN EMERALD, RUBY, AND DIAMOND BROOCH
by Cartier, Paris, 1957

Of heart-shaped design, *pavé*-set throughout with circular-cut diamonds, surmounted by a gold and *calibré*-cut ruby crown and applied at the centre with the initials W.E. in monogram set with *calibré*-cut emeralds above the roman numeral XX set with *calibré*-cut rubies, *maker's poinçon and numbered: 9479, one emerald deficient.*

The following weights are recorded in Cartier's archives: circular-cut diamonds: 5.92 carats.

To commemorate the Duke and Duchess of Windsor's twentieth wedding anniversary.

above
91. A GOLD CHAIN BRACELET
by Cartier

Of curb linking supporting a gold Latin cross, *inscribed in facsimile: God protect My darling David in his Going out & coming In from his loving G . . . Octr 26. 1921*; and a gold tear drop Pendant, *signed on the bolt ring, Cartier.*

The name of the donor, whose signature is inscribed on the Latin cross in this lot, is unfortunately impossible to decipher. It should be remembered, however, that the Prince's favourite at this time was Mrs Freda Dudley Ward, whom he had first met in 1918.

Edward, Prince of Wales, left Portsmouth in H.M.S. *Renown* on 26th October, 1921, bound for an extended tour of India and Japan, returning to Plymouth on 20th June the following year. The Duke subsequently remembered that at the start of the journey, 'My old tutor, Mr Hansel, now grown quite old, was on the dock to wave good-bye. In the late afternoon, with the crew fallen in and the band playing "Auld Lang Syne" against the booming of a salute of twenty-one guns, the battle-cruiser sailed. This time I was to be gone eight months . . . The East had always fascinated me. Ever since my tour of duty in Egypt during the war, I had longed to explore the lands that lay beyond the Red Sea.' [*A King's Story*. pp. 164/5.] See ill. 12.

overleaf
92. A DIAMOND BRACELET
by Cartier, circa 1935

Designed as a single row of spectacle-set brilliant-cut diamonds supporting nine gem-set Latin crosses, comprising: (1) in sapphire, emerald and diamond, *inscribed and dated: Our marriage Cross Wallis 3.VI.37 David, slightly imperfect*; (2) in aquamarine, *inscribed and dated: God save the King for Wallis 16.VII.36*; (3) in amethyst, *inscribed and dated: Appendectomy Cross Wallis 31.VIII.44 David*; (4) in emerald, *inscribed and dated: X Ray Cross Wallis – David 10.7.36*; (5) in baguette diamonds, *inscribed and dated: The Kings [sic] Cross God bless WE 1.3.36*; (6) in ruby, *inscribed and dated: Wallis – David St Wolfgang 22.9.3(5)*; (7) in yellow sapphire, *inscribed and dated: "Get Well" Cross Wallis Sept. 1944 David*; (8) in sapphire, *inscribed and dated: Wallis – David 23.6.35;* and (9) in platinum, *inscribed and dated: WE are too [sic] 25-XI-34.*

The following notes refer to the inscriptions engraved upon each cross. See ill. 93.

1. The Duke of Windsor and Wallis Simpson were married by the Rev. R. A Jardine on 3rd June, 1937, at the Château de Candé, Monts (Indre et Loire), France. The guests included Fern Bedaux, Herman Rogers and his wife, Katherine, Lady Alexandra Metcalfe, Mrs D. Buchanan Merryman (Mrs Simpson's Aunt Bessie), Dudley Forwood and Major E. D. ('Fruity') Metcalfe.

The Duchess in her memoirs remembered their wedding day: 'Somehow the preparations got done. Mainbocher made my trousseau. From his sketches I chose for my wedding gown a simple dress of blue crepe satin. Reboux made a hat to match. I asked Constance Spry, the prominent London florist, to come to Candé to do the flowers . . . [It] was beautifully warm and sunny. Herman Rogers gave me away, and it must have been with a profound sense of relief that he saw me become the responsibility of another.

'Here I shall say only that it was a supremely happy moment. All I had been through, the hurts I had suffered, were forgotten; by evening, David and I were on our way to Austria.' [*The Heart Has Its Reasons,* pp. 297/9.]

2. This inscription refers to an incident on 16th July, 1936, when King Edward VIII was riding in a procession on Constitution Hill after presenting new colours to the Guards. He was threatened by an Irish journalist named Macmahon with a loaded revolver. Mrs Simpson mentioned the fact, but only in passing and after giving details of her own health [see 4 below], in a letter to Aunt Bessie on 1st August: 'The shot [sic] at HM and the upset summer plans have all been very disturbing.' [*Letters,* p. 211.]

3. The Duchess of Windsor, who in the spring and summer of 1944 had been ailing for some months, left Nassau and was subsequently admitted to the Roosevelt Hospital, New York, where she underwent an operation for appendicitis with complications on 31st August [Michael Bloch, *The Duke of Windsor's War,* London, 1982, p. 342].

4. This cross was presented only a few days before King Edward VIII was threatened with a loaded revolver [see 2 above]. Mrs Simpson wrote from Fort Belvedere on 1st Au-

gust, 1936, to her Aunt Bessie giving details of her state of health: 'I had myself X-rayed from head to toes. They found a *healed* ulcer scar. I have an awfully good doctor and haven't had any trouble for 6 weeks. Have a diet – not too bad a one – the doctor is a German. I have gained some weight also, and feel better than I have for ages.' [*Letters,* p. 211.]

5. This inscription probably refers to the date of Mrs Simpson's departure for Paris on 1st March, 1936, when, after six exhausting weeks of the new reign, she sought, with her friend 'Foxy' Gwynne, a few days relaxation. It may be construed from the sentiment expressed on the charm that the King, still in mourning for his father and heavily burdened with unfamiliar duties, was not exactly pleased at her disappearance. For her part, Mrs Simpson seems to have been equally exasperated with the King, writing to her Aunt Bessie on 8th March that, although she had been invited to go on from Paris to Monte Carlo, 'that little King insists I return and I might as well with the telephone about 4 times daily – not much rest.' Meanwhile, apparently upon the initiative of Ernest Simpson, Mrs Simpson's absence gave the two men an opportunity of speaking frankly about their respective roles concerning her. At a meeting which is thought to have taken place during that first week in March, 'a private arrangement was reached between the King and Ernest, whereby Ernest agreed to put an end to his marriage with Wallis provided that the King promised to remain faithful to her and look after her.' [*Letters,* pp. 188-190.]

On a lighter note, the inscription brings to mind a contemporary tale about Mrs Simpson 'taking a taxi on her now famous journey to Scotland. "King's Cross", she is reported to have said. "I'm sorry, lady," answered the driver.' [Robert Rhodes James, editor, *Chips the Diaries of Sir Henry Channon,* London, 1967, p. 79, 11th November, 1936.]

6. See footnote to ill. 93 (2)

7. See note 3 above.

8. Edward, Prince of Wales' 41st birthday. See ills. 93 (1) and 207.

9. The inscription 'WE are too 25-XI-34' is a punning allusion to Mrs Simpson and the Prince of Wales' (WE) feelings for one another: WE (Wallis and Edward) are also in love, and WE two are in love. This is of particular significance as the Prince's brother, George, Duke of Kent, was married a few days later, on 29th November, 1934, to Princess Marina of Greece, at Westminster Abbey. See ill. 93 (3).

A *wedding photograph,*
1937, of the Duke and Duchess of Windsor. Note the
bracelet of crosses (ill. 92), the marriage contract bracelet
(ill. 106) and the Duchess of Windsor's wedding ring.

93. A GOLD CHAIN NECKLACE

Supporting: (1) a Ruby Pendant, designed as a Latin cross, the reverse inscribed and dated: *David – Wallis 23.6.35;* (2) a similar sapphire Latin cross Pendant, inscribed and dated on the reverse: *22.9.35 David – Wallis St Wolfgang, signed: Cartier, Paris;* and (3) another Latin cross Pendant, inscribed very indistinctly, possibly: *Wallis ?5 11 34.*

This necklace and the bracelet in ill. 92 with their inscribed Latin cross charms, became widely known at the time of the controversial *Nahlin* cruise in the Summer of 1936 from a number of photographs which appeared in the international press. These, clearly showing Wallis Simpson wearing the crosses around one of her wrists, caused intense speculation as to the true nature of the couple's relationship. Diana Cooper, a member of the King's party on that occasion, remembered that both the King and Mrs Simpson were seen to wear them. After joining the royal party along the Dalmatian coast, she wrote to her friend Conrad Russell: 'We . . . were greeted by the young King radiant in health, wearing spick-and-span little shorts, straw sandals and two [*sic*] crucifixes on a chain round his neck . . .' [Diana Cooper, *The Light of Common Day*, London, 1959, p. 175; Philip Ziegler, *Diana Cooper*, London, 1981, p. 176.] The King's were those seen here; Mrs Simpson's those in ill. 92.

In February, 1937, by which time Mrs Simpson was staying at Cannes and the Duke at the Schloss Enzesfeld in Austria, she wrote to him enclosing 'proofs of [Cecil] Beaton's article that is going to appear in US *Vogue*. See about the crosses and the cairn in the article.' [*Letters*, p. 277.] The piece duly appeared [1st July, 1937, pp.32-35], but only after their wedding on 3rd June and in a version in which the crosses were no longer mentioned.

1. Mrs Simpson's gift to the Prince of Wales to commemorate his forty-first birthday. See ills. 92 (8) and 207.

2. In his autobiography [*A King's Story*, pp. 258/9], the Duke of Windsor wrote of the time in 1935 when, by reason of his father the King's failing health, he was forced to look to his own future and that of his con-

nection with the Crown. 'I could not discount,' he wrote, 'the possibility of my having to withdraw altogether from the line of succession if my hope [of marrying Wallis] were ever to be fulfilled.' Although the Prince fully intended to discuss the matter with his father, the moment never seemed propitious: that summer of 1935 saw the King, 'off as usual for Balmoral and me on a shooting trip in Austria and Hungary.'

The Prince of Wales, who was joined on this two months' holiday by a few close friends including Wallis Simpson, went with his party from Cannes on 9th September via a number of destinations, returning on 2nd October to Paris and thence by aeroplane to Windsor. According to Mrs Simpson, who had written to her aunt from the Carlton Hotel in Cannes on 7th September, they expected to 'leave Monday for Budapest, 1 day on the train and 2 nights. We shall stay in Budapest until the week-end and then go to some place on a lake for the week-end and then I think motor to Vienna perhaps a touch of the Austrian Tyrol and Paris . . .' [*Letters*, p. 157]. On the way, between 20th and 24th September, 1935, they stayed not far from Salzburg at the small town of St. Wolfgang [*A King's Story*, p. 423]. Why the visit to this place should have been remarkable enough for Prince Edward and Mrs Simpson to commemorate it with gifts of crosses to each other is unknown. The reason, as for so much of the jewellery in the Duchess's collection, was clearly very personal; indeed, the holiday may well have marked a decisive moment in their relationship and, as Michael Bloch has noted [*Letters*, p. 159], when the Prince of Wales returned to England, 'the idea of marriage to her had become a fixed and passionate desire.' See ill. 92 (6).

3. See ill. 92 (9).

94. AN INTERESTING COLLECTION OF TWELVE CHARMS

Including: (1) a hinged envelope, inscribed on the front: *TELEGRAM E. P.* and inscribed inside: *no zig zags;* (2) a cushion-shaped plaque decorated with a red enamel figure 3 and dated on the reverse: *9/4/34 march 12th 1934 14/5/34;* (3) a hinged notebook, the interior decorated with the initials D and W in red and blue enamel and dated: *June 1934 1st-4th;* (4) another cushion-shaped plaque, inscribed and dated: *Hello! 18/5/34 22/5/34? [sic] 28/8/34*; (5) a medallion representing the letters OK, the reverse inscribed: *I doo too July [sic]*; (6) another cushion-shaped plaque inscribed: *Run Along*, the reverse dated: *11/9/34 21/9/34*; (7) a locket dated: *April '35*, the interior with a hair compartment and inscribed: *Wallis – David*; (8) a ladybird, *by Cartier, London*, set with diamonds and inscribed: *David 4/12/36 Wallis, signed: Cartier, London*; (9) a heart, *by Cartier*, decorated with the words and signs: *+ qu'hier – que demain*, in blue and white enamel, the reverse inscribed and dated: *David Thumb 1944, signed: Cartier*; (10) a frog; (11) a hairpin; (12) the initials E W inscribed: *October*; all on a chain Necklet. The following notes refer to some of the charms seen here.

4. The significance of the dates 18th and 22nd May, 1934, is not clear, although they would appear to coincide with Mrs Simpson's stay at Fort Belvedere as one of the Prince of Wales' Ascot week house guests [*Letters*, pp. 114/5]. On 28th August, the Prince and Mrs Simpson and her aunt Mrs Bessie Merryman were staying at Biarritz. See (6) below.

6. The months of August and September, 1934, saw Mrs Simpson and her aunt, together with a small group of friends, as the Prince of Wales' holiday guests. Leaving Paris on 1st August, they stayed at a villa in Biarritz from 2nd to 30th of the month, before leaving for a Mediterranean cruise in Lord Iveagh's yacht, *Rosaura*, which lasted until 23rd September. In *The Heart Has Its Reasons* [p. 197], the Duchess of Windsor wrote that one evening in Cannes, 'after we had been with Herman and Katherine Rogers for dinner, the Prince took from his pocket a tiny velvet case and put it into my hand. It contained a little diamond and emerald charm for my bracelet.' See (4) above.

7. The fair hair contained in this locket is of the same colour as that of Edward, Prince of Wales. 'Accompanied by their friends the Hunters, Wallis and Ernest spent Easter [1935] motoring with the Prince around his estates in Cornwall. It was during this trip that the Prince wrote the first of his letters to Wallis which appears to have survived. It is no more than a *billet doux* accompanying a present to her; but it suggests that there had already been much correspondence between them . . . ' [*Letters*, p. 138].

8. This charm, echoing the children's nursery rhyme, 'Ladybird, ladybird, fly away home,' and its inscription probably refer to some incident during Mrs Simpson's harrowing journey from London to Cannes which was undertaken between 3rd and 6th December, 1936. For further comment, see ill. 114.

9. The enamel inscription probably refers to the oft-used phrase, 'more and more and more'.

10. 'My Sweetheart,' wrote the Duke of Windsor to Mrs Simpson from Schloss Enzesfeld on 26th January, 1937, during their enforced separation, ' . . . I enclose an eanum frog for the thirty first to live in your bag with the fat Vienna frog . . . Please show the new eanum frog to HER as HE has seen it! How HE longs for house and make soon HE says too. God bless WE my beloved Wallis. Remember what the eanum frog says and that I love you more and more . . . ' To which Wallis responded, 'I love the new frog and so does "she" the diamond nearly put her eye out!' [*Letters*, pp.271/ 4.]

11. The following references in correspondence of Edward, Prince of Wales, later Duke of Windsor, and Mrs Simpson, to hair pins have been noted.

The Prince to Mrs Simpson from the Fort, June, 1935: 'Oh! so many happy returns my sweetheart and God bless WE for ever. More and more and more we all of us say. HE is terribly excited about new hair pin and HE hopes SHE is too . . . ' [*Letters*, p. 148.]

The Duke of Windsor to Mrs Simpson from Schloss Enzesfeld, 1st January, 1937: 'Hello! my sweetheart. Such a very happy New Year I wish for WE for the fastness of my "exile" . . . Oh! poor everybody WE all say and HE is so scared of loosing [sic] his hairpin that he does want HER to hurry and send him another to secure the old one . . . ' [*Letters*, p. 263.]

The Duke of Windsor to Mrs Simpson from Lou Viei, Cannes, 3rd January, 1937: 'Darling Sweetheart . . . "She" sends the hairpin which "she" says she found very comfortable and hopes "he" will . . . " [*Letters*, p.267.]

95. A PAIR OF GOLD AND RUBY PINS
by Van Cleef & Arpels, New York

Each with a trefoil terminal, star-set with brilliant-cut rubies and with a larger ruby claw-set at the centre, *each signed and numbered: V. C. A. N. Y. 3058.*

According to the archives of Van Cleef & Arpels, New York, a pair of hatpins, numbered 3058 and 5679, were a gift to the Duchess of Windsor from Louis Arpels, a director of the firm.

96. A PAIR OF GOLD AND RUBY EARCLIPS
by Cartier, Paris, circa 1945

Each designed as a cluster of ruby beads surmounted by a gold corded wire fan motif, *signed and numbered: Cartier 01373*; and a matching Earclip, *signed and numbered: Cartier Paris 01373.*

97. AN 18 CARAT GOLD
AND GEM-SET CIGARETTE CASE
by Cartier, London, 1935

Rectangular, the front decorated with a map of Europe in yellow and red gold, inscribed with the names of various locations, each represented by a cabochon gem or a brilliant-cut diamond, and connected by red and blue enamel lines, *the interior inscribed and dated: David from Wallis Christmas 1935, signed: Cartier, London, one stone deficient; 200 gms approximately.*

The enamelled routes on this and the jewelled compact (ill. 98) refer to holidays enjoyed by Prince Edward and his guests, including Mrs Simpson, during 1934, 1935 and 1936. Because of the date of the inscription on the cigarette case, it must be assumed that the route outlining the Balkan journey of the latest year was added some time after the box's original presentation.

In her memoirs, the Duchess explained that she and her Aunt Bessie Merryman, in the absence of Ernest Simpson who was going to America, had first been asked by the Prince of Wales to join him and a few friends on a trip abroad, which commenced with nearly a month's stay at Meremont, a villa in Biarritz. After this, from 1st to 17th September, the Prince and his party spent much of the time on Lord Moyne's yacht, *Rosaura.* According to the engraving on the cases, they moved from Biarritz on to Coruna (*sic*) and from there to Oporto, Arenas Gordas, Palma and Formentor before reaching Calvi in Corsica. They then returned to the mainland at Cannes, staying there from 11th to 16th of September, before going on to Genoa, Milan, Como, Vallorbe and finally via Paris back to Fort Belvedere in Windsor Great Park.

Early in the New Year, on 14th January, 1935, Mrs Simpson told Mrs Merryman that, 'The Prince is thinking of going to Kitzbuhl in February and has invited Foxy Gwynne, Lord Dudley, Captain and Mrs Bruce Ogilvy . . . To be gone 2 weeks – if it comes off . . .' When Wallis Simpson spoke of this to her husband, telling him that the Prince wanted them both along, he greeted the news coolly, saying he had no interest in skiing and anyway was due to be in New York at that time. Mrs Simpson paid little attention to Mr Simpson's annoyance; she, the Prince and party left London on 4th February, travelling via Calais to Kitzbuhl in the Austrian Tyrol where they stayed at the Grand Hotel from 5th to 17th. A letter from there to

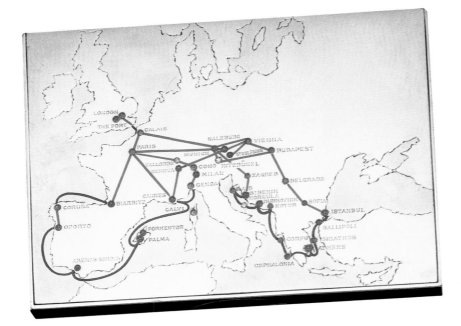

Mrs Merryman outlined the itinerary for the remainder of the holiday: '. . . 10 days here, 3 days Vienna, 3 days Budapest, Paris, home.' Again, the engraving on the cases confirms this route. When Mrs Simpson arrived back in London, her aunt heard that, 'The trip was a great success and Budapest the best part, such a gay amusing place. 2 days in Paris where I bought a couple of hats . . . I was very interested in the clippings. What the US papers don't put on to this poor Prince . . . I wish you had sent me clippings about the diamond and my glass coat. I have a small diamond that clips into my hair which HRH gave me and the coat is cellophane.'

Regarding the summer holiday of that year of 1935, Mrs Merryman received advance warning in a letter of 16th July. 'The Prince has taken [Lord Cholmonde-ley's] villa at Cannes from August – has his own rocks and will rent a boat.' Ernest Simpson again did not accompany his wife. As related in the Duchess's memoirs, the Prince's party 'took a cruise [from Cannes] on the Duke of Westminster's yacht, *Cutty Sark*, to Corsica; later Daisy Fellowes lent us her yacht, *Sister Anne*, for a cruise along the coast as far as the island of Porquerolles.'

'Not unexpectedly,' continued the Duchess regarding their stay at Cannes, 'David decided one day that we ought to revisit the delights of Vienna and Budapest, taken this time in reverse order.' During this trip, from 20th until 24th September, they stayed at St. Wolfgang [ill. 93 (2)], before returning to England in early October.

The final holiday recorded on the cases is that of the summer of 1936, about which the Duke of Windsor subsequently wrote: 'It had long been my habit as Prince of Wales to spend a part of the summer holidays abroad . . . And now that I was King, I saw no reason for abandoning this agreeable and enriching practice . . .' Taking up the story, the Duchess remembered that, having chartered Lady Yule's yacht, the *Nahlin*, the King, 'decided to explore new waters – the Dalmation

[sic] Coast, Greece and the Aegean Isles, and the Bosphorus. His hope was to recapture the carefree spirit of our last two summers . . .' But the cruise was not an unqualified success; both host and guests were to recollect it with mixed feelings. For one thing, the King and Mrs Simpson's relationship had now become the cause of intense speculation and they were mobbed everywhere by crowds of sightseers as well as representatives of the American and Continental press.

At Istanbul, where Edward VIII met the Turkish dictator Ataturk, the travellers left the *Nahlin*, heading northwards overland via Sofia and Belgrade once more towards Budapest and Vienna. 'A pleasant five days in that most charming of capitals – Vienna,' the Duke recalled later, 'wound up my holiday . . . I continued westward across Europe with my party in the Orient Express. My own aeroplane met me at Zurich; and with an equerry I flew home, to resume my duties and to deal with a personal problem which it had become increasingly clear could not be held much longer in abeyance.' Mrs Simpson, meanwhile, together with the remaining *Nahlin* guests, spent a few days in Paris before returning to England. [*Letters*, pp. 132-136, 149, 151, 152, 157, 212-215, 322; *The Heart Has Its Reasons*, pp. 195, 217, 228-233; *A King's Story*, pp. 305-310, 423/4; Cecil Beaton, *The Wandering Years*, London, 1961, p. 308.] See ills. 21 and 98.

opposite
98. AN 18 CARAT GOLD AND GEM-SET POWDER COMPACT
French, circa 1936

Of lunette design, the front *pavé*-set with various gems including: sapphire, ruby, emerald, citrine, amethyst, etc., the reverse decorated with a map of Europe inscribed with various locations connected by red or blue enamel lines, *enamel imperfect, maker's poinçon indistinct, suede pochette by Hermès-Paris*; and an 18 carat gold on gem-set lipstick case, *en suite*, the two terminals similarly set, *French. See note to ill. 97.*

99. AN ONYX POCKET WATCH
by Cartier, circa 1936

Designed as a rectangular onyx plaque, the similarly shaped dial at the centre, the reverse with the cypher of Edward VIII, *the winding crown inscribed: Easter 12/ 4/36; suede leather pochette by Cartier.*

The Prince of Wales, who had succeeded his father as King on 20th January, 1936, spent Easter that year with Mrs Simpson at Fort Belvedere together with a few guests [*Letters*, p. 321]. Writing to her Aunt, she was able to report on 14th April upon her return to Bryanston Court, 'We had a very quiet Easter party at the Fort with people from about the neighbourhood for dinner and Saturday HM had a film at Windsor Castle. That is his form of amusement these days, having films either there or in York House—a slight contact with the outside world costing a bit, but he is very rich now.' [*Letters*, p. 194.]

100. A GOLD POCKET WATCH
by Cartier, Paris

Of oval form, the glazed circular watch face with roman chapters, *signed Cartier, inscribed in facsimile beneath: No excuse for going in the Wrong direction Easter 1939,* the reverse set with a compass and engraved with a sundial, *inscribed on the edge: Made in France.*

It was early in 1939 that the Duke and Duchess of Windsor, having previously hoped to return to live in England, finally found a house in Paris which suited their needs. 'It was on the Boulevard Suchet,' so wrote the Duchess, 'at the end of Avenue Henri Martin, not far from the Bois de Boulogne . . . [It] was airy and sunny, in the Louis Seize style, with windows all around and a charming courtyard, and when I showed it to

David he smiled and said, "I see that it's going to be the city for us, after all."' [*The Heart Has Its Reasons*, p. 315.]

opposite
101. AN ENAMEL, RUBY AND DIAMOND EVENING BAG
circa 1930

The front of the frame decorated with black enamel dart and scroll motifs, *pavé*-set throughout with brilliant-cut diamonds and with diamond tipped ruby beads at intervals, the wedge-shaped pull similarly set, the reverse decorated with star-set rubies and diamonds, the pink and gold bag embroidered in a design of foliate and stylised flowerhead motifs on an ivory-coloured ground; satin purse.

102. A GOLD AQUAMARINE AND RUBY SCENT FLACON
by Van Cleef & Arpels, New York

Engraved with flowerspray motifs, the stopper set with an aquamarine briolette and a band of cushion-shaped rubies, *the base signed and numbered: Van Cleef & Arpels N.Y. 12940, case.*

opposite
103. A PAIR OF STAINED BLUE CHALCEDONY, SAPPHIRE AND DIAMOND BANGLES
probably by Belperron, circa 1935

Each in a ridged coronet design, the front set with seven brilliant-cut diamonds each surmounted by a stained blue chalcedony bead capped with a cabochon sapphire.

Amongst the most revolutionary jewellery designers of the 1920's and '30's, Suzanne Belperron subsequently opened a shop called Herz-Belperron in the Rue Châteaudun, Paris. The Duchess of Windsor is known to have frequented Madame Belperron's establishment. See American *Vogue*, 15th November, 1937, p. 77.

104. A STAINED BLUE CHALCEDONY, SAPPHIRE AND DIAMOND NECKLACE
probably by Belperron, circa 1935

Designed as two rows of stained blue chalcedony beads on a large carved stained chalcedony flowerhead clasp, the centre set with a cluster of cabochon sapphires and bands of brilliant-cut diamonds.

105. A PAIR OF STAINED BLUE CHALCEDONY, SAPPHIRE AND DIAMOND EARCLIPS
probably by Belperron, circa 1935

Each designed as a foliate motif, the chalcedony leaf set with a tapered band of brilliant-cut diamonds and surmounted by a cluster of cabochon sapphires and circular-cut diamonds.

The Duchess of Windsor
photographed by Karsh of Ottawa wearing the chalcedony
necklace and earrings (ills. 104 and 105).

Sapphires

The sapphire has been prized since antiquity for the transparency of its beautiful deep-blue colour akin to the bloom of the humble cornflower. Like the ruby, of which they constitute a chemical equivalent, sapphires are formed from corundum, an oxide of aluminium, with minute traces in its composition of other metallic oxides. The red variety of the material is invariably known as ruby, whereas all others, not only blue, are called sapphires. Hues other than blue and pure white range from yellow and green to purple and grey, and while few are perfectly clear, some contain inclusions that, when cut and polished as cabochons, display a remarkable six-rayed star or asterism. Despite their hardness, sapphires are occasionally engraved, as in ill. 148. A fifty-three carat sapphire once owned by the Marchese Rinuccini is so decorated, with an elaborate hunting scene.

Fine sapphires, which are usually larger than rubies and not as rare or valuable, traditionally came from Cashmere in Northern India, but very few have been mined there within living memory. The principal sources now are Australia and Sri Lanka (Ceylon), the latter long famous for its abundance of precious and semi-precious stones, while also especially noted for rubies as well as blue and fancy coloured sapphires. Among the earliest traders with the island were the Chinese, who distinguished it as Pa-ou-tchow, the 'isle of gems'. Sinbad and Marco Polo head the long list of other romantic visitors in search of Sri Lanka's natural treasures. In more modern times, under British rule, the ancient monopoly in digging for gems enjoyed by the Kandyan Kings was abolished. The south-east was always the most productive gem-bearing quarter of the island, especially around Ratnapur, the 'City of Gems', with its surroundings of forest-flanked mountains cleft by rivers and waterfalls.

opposite part-title page
106. A SAPPHIRE AND DIAMOND *JARRETIÈRE* BRACELET
by Van Cleef & Arpels, Paris, 1937

Designed as a wide flexible band of baguette and circular-cut diamonds, the clasp of stylized bow design invisibly-set with cushion-shaped sapphires and baguette diamonds, *inscribed in facsimile: For our Contract 18-V-37; signed and numbered: Van Cleef & Arpels – Paris – 46923.*

Designed by René-Sim Lacaze for the Paris house of Van Cleef & Arpels whose archives record that the bracelet was purchased by the Duke of Windsor in May, 1937.

On 22nd March, 1937, the Duke wrote from the Schloss Enzesfeld to Mrs Simpson that he hated 'the waste of these four and a half months of our lives which are so vital and precious to us and which we'll never get back. Oh! poo when I think of it . . .'. He was, however, able to report that he had to hand, 'a copy relating to the formalities in France for our marriage,' continuing, 'Ooh! how lovely that sounds and you'll see what we have to do.' The inscription on this bracelet, a wedding gift from the Duke of Windsor to his bride, is connected with these formalities; their marriage contract was completed at Monts (Indre-et-Loire), France, on 18th May, 1937. [*Letters*, pp. 298/9.]

The photographs by Cecil Beaton of the Duchess in her wedding outfit clearly show her wearing the bracelet. [Cecil Beaton, 'Wedding of the Duke and Duchess of Windsor', *Vogue*, American edition, 1st May, 1937, pp. 32-35].

A *wedding photograph by Cecil Beaton, 1937, of the Duke and Duchess of Windsor at a window of the Château de Candé, France. Note the marriage contract bracelet (ill. 106).*

below: 107. An original design from Van Cleef & Arpels' Paris archives for the sapphire and diamond marriage contract bracelet (ill. 106). The design was subsequently modified.

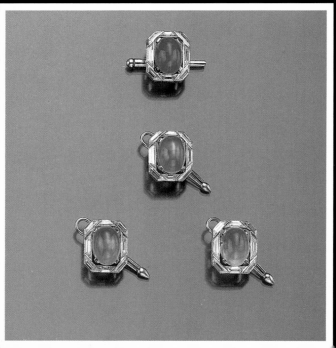

108. A SAPPHIRE BRACELET
by Cartier, circa 1945

Designed as a chain of eight open oval links set with cushion-shaped sapphires in alternating light and dark shades of blue, *signed on the clasp: Cartier.*

See Diana Mosley, *The Duchess of Windsor,* London, 1980, p. 171, a photograph of the Duchess wearing this bracelet at the Paris Horse Show in 1949.

109. A SUITE OF THREE STAR SAPPHIRE AND DIAMOND BUTTONS
by Van Cleef & Arpels, Paris

Each with a cabochon sapphire mounted within an octagonal border of trapeze-shaped diamonds; and a Stud, *en suite, one of the buttons and the stud signed and numbered: Van Cleef & Arpels Paris 31469.*

The Duke and Duchess of Windsor on the terrace of their house in Paris. Note the sapphire link bracelet (ill. 108).

110. A PAIR OF SAPPHIRE AND DIAMOND EARCLIPS
by Van Cleef & Arpels, New York, 1944

Each designed as a flowerhead cluster, the centre set with brilliant-cut diamonds, within a border of cushion-shaped sapphires and smaller similarly shaped rubies, *the clasp signed and numbered: Van Cleef & Arpels N.Y. 6104.*

According to the archives of Van Cleef & Arpels, New York, these earclips, numbered 6104, were made in 1944 and purchased in 1947.

111. A RUBY AND SAPPHIRE BROOCH
by Cartier, London, probably 1936

Designed as the initials W. E. entwined in *calibré*-cut sapphires and rubies, *signed: Cartier, London.*

The initials W. E. are those of Mrs Wallis Simpson and the Prince of Wales, later Edward VIII (Wallis and Edward), in a form symbolizing their union in love.

112. AN INVISIBLY SET SAPPHIRE RING
by Van Cleef & Arpels, New York, 1950

Of *bombé* form, the front with five tapered rows of sapphire, *the shank signed and numbered: Van Cleef & Arpels, N.Y. 17440.*

According to the archives of Van Cleef & Arpels, New York, this ring, numbered 17440, was made in 1950 and purchased by Mrs James Donahue. See note to ill. 172.

113. AN 18 CARAT GOLD SAPPHIRE AND DIAMOND PIN
by Van Cleef & Arpels, New York

The swivel head designed as a spherical cluster of sapphire beads with brilliant-cut diamonds set at intervals, *the pin signed and numbered: Van Cleef & Arpels N.Y. 5639.*

114. AN 18 CARAT YELLOW GOLD, PLATINUM, RUBY AND SAPPHIRE DRESS RING
by Cartier, Paris, 1937

Of turban design, set with three tapered rows of cushion-shaped rubies and three similar bands of sapphires, *the shank inscribed and dated: Our Reunion in Candé 3-XII-36–3-V-37, the bezel signed and numbered: Cartier, Paris 03738.*

The inscription refers to the period of Edward VIII and Mrs Simpson's separation upon the crisis of their possible marriage becoming public in England when she fled to Cannes on 3rd December, 1936: 'On the night of Wednesday 2 December – which was cold and foggy – the King took [Mrs Simpson] for a stroll on the terrace of the Fort after dinner. He told her of his interview with [Prime Minister] Baldwin that day, which seemed to leave no choice between abdication and renunciation of her, the second of which courses was unthinkable to him . . . The following morning the storm broke. All the newspapers were full of the royal marriage issue, and the general tone was one of disapproval . . . Wallis's journey to Cannes was nightmarish . . . No sooner had they [Mrs Simpson together with the King's old friend and Lord-in-Waiting, Lord ('Perry') Brownlow, and Inspector Evans of Scotland Yard] disembarked in France than Wallis – in spite of the measures which had been taken to keep her journey secret – began to be recognized; and before long an army of newshounds were on her trail. As the party tried to shake them off, a fantastic flight ensued, with sudden changes of route, frantic near-encounters with their pursuers, and hurried, clandestine departures from hotels and restaurants. Throughout the two days they spent on the road under these agitated circumstances, Wallis (who allowed herself to be guided by Brownlow) was in a state of mounting anxiety over the fate of the King . . . Finally, at two o'clock on the morning of Sunday 6 December, their Buick – with the King's chauffeur Ladbrook at the wheel – drove past the crowd of reporters who had discovered their destination and through the gates of Lou Viei, the Rogers' villa, Wallis crouching on the floor of the car with a rug over her head.' [*Letters*, pp. 237-241.]

The date of 3rd May, 1937, in the inscription refers to the news of the final chapter in Mrs Simpson's divorce from her husband, Ernest, which made way for her reunion with the Duke of Windsor:

'Finally, on the morning of May 3, there was a telephone call from George Allen [the Duke of Windsor's solicitor] in London. My divorce decree had now be-

come absolute. I telephoned David in Austria. "Wallis," he said, "the Orient Express passes through Salzburg in the afternoon. I shall be at Candé in the morning"... David arrived at lunch time [on the 4th] with his equerry Dudley Forwood..." [*The Heart Has Its Reasons*, p. 296.]

opposite
115. A SAPPHIRE AND DIAMOND NECKLACE
by Cartier, circa 1940

Designed as two rows of sapphire beads supporting nine articulated flowerhead clusters, graduating in size from the centre, set with cabochon sapphires and circular-cut diamonds, and decorated with dart-shaped drops set with circular-cut diamonds, *makers' poinçon*.

116. A SAPPHIRE AND DIAMOND CLIP
by Cartier, Paris, 1949

Designed as an elaborate ribbon bow of oval-shaped sapphires and circular-cut diamonds, the knot set with a rosette cluster of similarly cut stones, *signed and numbered on the Clip: Cartier, Paris, 010241*. The following weights are recorded in Cartier's archives: fifty-six sapphires: 223.24 carats; fifty-three brilliant-cut diamonds: 7.61 carats.

117. A SAPPHIRE AND DIAMOND RING
by Cartier, Paris, 1949

The larger circular-cut sapphire set within a border of smaller similarly cut sapphires between diamond shoulders, on a platinum shank, *signed and numbered: Cartier, Paris, M 8044*. The following weights are recorded in Cartier's archives: circular sapphire: 46.60 carats; thirty-six sapphires: 14.92 carats; forty-four diamonds: 2.14 carats.

A photograph by Patrick
Lichfield of the Duchess of Windsor and Mrs Aileen
Plunkett dressed in identical gowns by Givenchy. Note the
sapphire and diamond pendant (ill. 119) worn with the
diamond rivière (ill. 204), and the sapphire and diamond
earrings (ill. 118).

118. A PAIR OF SAPPHIRE
AND DIAMOND PENDANT EARCLIPS
probably by Cartier

Each with a drop-shaped cabochon sapphire suspended from a diamond-set surmount designed as stylised Prince of Wales' feathers, *makers' poinçon rubbed, numbered indistinctly: P 8338 and P 8438.*

This pair of sapphires weighing 75.51 carats were purchased from Harry Winston on 16th April, 1947, mounted as earclips. It is understood that they were subsequently re-set by Cartier; they now weigh 75.33 carats, probably as a result of re-polishing.

119. A SAPPHIRE AND DIAMOND PENDANT
by Cartier, Paris, 1951

The cushion-shaped sapphire claw-set within a border of baguette and brilliant-cut diamonds, the detachable loop set with two rows of baguette diamonds; brooch fitting; *makers' poinçon.* The following weights are recorded in Cartier's archives: cushion-shaped sapphire: 206.82 carats; diamonds: 11.31 carats.

Emerals

A silicate of beryllium and aluminium, the emerald is found naturally in six-sided prisms or columns in colour shading from grass-green to greenish-white. They owe their particularly beautiful hue to the presence of chromium, ironically the same metal that gives rise to the 'pigeon-blood' red of the Burmese ruby. The relatively flawless emerald of good colour, of which that in the Duchess of Windsor's engagement ring is a very fine example (ill. 120), is among the world's rarest gemstone.

In the ancient world emeralds were much valued as in Egypt where they were all considered to be royal property. Cleopatra, it is said, even had portraits of herself engraved upon them for presentation to favoured ambassadors. Although emeralds are found in other parts of the world, by far the most valuable have been mined in South America, an important source ever since the 1560's. Indeed, recent investigators are of the opinion that many of the famous stones owned by the former Marharajas of India, who had a great penchant for the gem, were originally exported from that region.

The Duchess of Windsor
photographed by Cecil Beaton, probably at Candé in
1937, wearing her engagement ring (ill 120).

120. AN EMERALD AND DIAMOND RING
mounted by Cartier, Paris, 1958

Set with a rectangular step-cut emerald with cut corners weighing 19.77 carats within a stylized leaf border set with brilliant-cut diamonds, *inscribed: Monture Cartier; together with the original emerald ring mount by Cartier, London, 1936, inscribed in facsimile in the shank: We are ours now 27 X 36; and signed: Cartier, London.*

This emerald, remounted in its present setting by Cartier in Paris in 1958, was purchased from the same firm in London in 1936 by Edward VIII as Wallis Simpson's engagement ring. The platinum ring mount included in this lot was originally set with the large emerald remounted by Cartier in 1958. The 27th October, 1936, marked by the King and Mrs Simpson with this ring as their engagement day, was also that upon which the proceedings of her divorce from Ernest Simpson were heard in Ipswich. Mrs Simpson, who had been obliged to stay with friends at Felixstowe nearby, returned the same evening to London. [For further information, see *Letters*, chapter 9.]

In her diary for 1st June, 1939, Marie Belloc Lowndes records an interesting conversation concerning the stone she had 'with the great jeweller', Jacques Cartier, while lunching at Margot Asquith's. 'We began talking about the Duchess of Windsor,' she wrote. 'I said that I supposed he [Cartier] knew her very well. He said though he did know her, he had not come across her often, and that she had a great many fine jewels, including an engagement ring given to her by King Edward VIII—which is one of the greatest emeralds in the world and belonged to the Grand Mogul. In those days it was as large as a bird's egg, and in connection with this he told me the following story:

'Cartier's heard that certain people in Baghdad were anxious to sell their jewels but that it would take some time as they were not allowed to do so, and it would all have to be done secretly. Cartier's sent out one of their most trusted emissaries. After he had been there for some time he telegraphed home for a very large sum of money: they were taken aback but thought that he must be on the point of procuring an enormous number of precious stones. They sent him the money and

awaited his return with great excitement. When he arrived they were surprised to see that he had with him only a little bag, and to their increasing dismay, out of it he brought this immense emerald. Their dismay increased for, as they pointed out to him, there was no one in the world—now that the old Russia had been destroyed—who would give a large enough price for it to make a profit. He then suggested that it should be cut in half and re-polished. This was accordingly done, making the two most splendid emeralds in the world. One was bought in due course by an American millionaire—the other by the King.' [Susan Lowndes, editor, *Diaries and Letters of Marie Belloc Lowndes*, London, 1971, p. 177.]

121. AN EMERALD AND DIAMOND NECKLACE
mounted by Cartier, Paris, 1960

The front in the design of five pear-shaped clusters, each set at the centre with a pear-shaped emerald within a radiated border of baguette and marquise diamonds, the sides and back designed as a line of semicircular links set with circular- and square-cut diamonds, *the diamond cluster clasp inscribed: Monture Cartier P 6655; the central cluster fitted with a loop to support the emerald and diamond pendant, lot 79.*

The following weights are recorded in Cartier's archives; principal emerald: 14.61 carats; four pear-shaped emeralds: 5.82, 6.61, 6.67 and 7.82 carats; one hundred and ten baguette diamonds: 28.01 carats; eighteen navette diamonds: 13.49 carats; one hundred and seventy-six brilliant-cut diamonds: 24.76 carats.

122. AN EMERALD AND DIAMOND PENDANT
by Harry Winston, 1960

The large pear-shaped emerald claw-set within a border of navette and circular-cut diamonds, *the pendant can be worn as the central drop of the necklace, or as a clip; clip fitting by Cartier.* The weights supplied at the date of purchase by Harry Winston are as follows: pear-shaped emerald: 48.95 carats; nine marquise diamonds: 4.68 carats; thirteen round diamonds: 3.83 carats.

A file copy of a letter dated 27th May, 1960, preserved in the late Duchess of Windsor's archives, writ-

The Duchess of Windsor wearing the emerald and diamond earclips, pendant and necklace (ills. 121, 122 and 123).

ten by Michael I. McAlister, M. A., A. C. A., private secretary to H.R.H. the Duke of Windsor, and addressed to Harry Winston in New York, mentions this jewel in the following terms: '. . . His Royal Highness tells me that it was agreed between yourself and their Royal Highnesses that you would accept the Duchess' two Emerald & Diamond necklaces in exchange for the Pear-shaped Emerald Pendant which you delivered to the Duke and Duchess aboard S.S. "United States".' In his reply of 9th June, 1960, Mr. Winston expressed his own estimation of the stone: 'Not only because of

its intrinsic value as a fine emerald, but since it had once belonged to the late King of Spain [Alphonso XIII] naturally enhances its value considerably [*sic*].'

overleaf, left to right: ills. 123, 124 and 125.

123. AN EMERALD AND DIAMOND CLIP
mounted by Cartier, Paris, 1948

Designed as a step-cut emerald, and a similarly cut diamond, connected by a zigzag pattern of trapeze-shaped stones, inscribed: *For Our Mondays and their Maundy Anniversery [sic] 9.4.36, and: Wallis! Hello eanum pig 1934;* signed and numbered: *Monture Cartier, 1/7315.* The following weights are recorded in Cartier's archives: step-cut diamond: 3.32 carats; step-cut emerald: 2.80 carats; two *calibré*-cut emeralds: 1.02 carats; two baguette diamonds: 0.87 carat.

The presence of two separate inscriptions, respectively dated 1934 and 1936, on this Cartier brooch of 1948, suggests that its stones were previously mounted in two different settings. If this supposition is correct, it is likely that both jewels were gifts to mark a similar event. With the reference to Maundy Thursday, 1936, this could have been the festival of Easter, a point on the calendar held as special by both the Prince of Wales and Mrs Simpson.

Easter, 1935, like several others in later years, was certainly commemorated by a royal present for Mrs Simpson. This was the occasion when the Prince wrote to her, 'My Eanum—My Wallis . . . The Easter Bunny has brought this from Us All & Slipper says he likes it too but it has to be fitted & christened later . . . ' No description of the gift is included, but Mrs Simpson herself seems to hint at its valuable nature in a letter of 29th April, a few days later, to Mrs Merryman: 'I have some lovely jewellery to show when we meet. Not many things but awfully nice stones . . . ' [*Letters*, pp. 138/9.]

'Eanum pigs' were a part of the Duke of Windsor and Mrs Simpson's private vocabulary, as in his letter to her of 22nd December, 1936: HE (I hide face) Eanum and Pig (I hide face again) and all the toys miss YOU ALL at LOO VIEI more than they can say,' and again when, on 22nd March, 1937, he sent her a packet of

153

Gunsebrust with the advice, 'don't make eanum pig.' [*Letters*, pp. 258 and 300.]

The meaning of the other inscription is less easy to account for. Both 'our' and 'their' are probably allusions to donor and recipient, the King and Mrs Simpson, in much the same way as the initials WE symbolised their love for one another. The perverse linking of the words 'monday' and 'maundy' (the latter meaning the special alms traditionally awarded annually by the reigning monarch to chosen pensioners on the Thursday before Easter) is simply a pun.

Mondays, in particular those spent in 1934 and '35 at Fort Belvedere together, appear to have been important to the lovers; the death of King George V on 20th January, 1936, and the subsequent accession of the Prince of Wales to the throne were events which were to shatter the relative peace of their lives forever. In a letter from the Fort to Aunt Bessie Merryman on Monday, 14th October, 1935, Mrs Simpson explained the significance of the first day of the week when she and the Prince were usually left to themselves, his other guests of the week-end having departed: 'I live such an

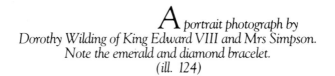

A *portrait photograph by
Dorothy Wilding of King Edward VIII and Mrs Simpson.
Note the emerald and diamond bracelet.
(ill. 124)*

abnormal life these days never having a second to my-self that writing is impossible except Monday morning here when the Prince is out cutting down everything in sight.' Many of Mrs Simpson's letters to her aunt while staying at the Fort were written on Mondays [*Letters*, pp. 161/2, et seq.]; the reference to the Prince 'cutting down everything in sight,' is to his clearing the Fort's grounds of undergrowth, a form of recreation he found especially appealing [*A King's Story*, p. 237].

Thursday, 9th April, 1936, as the inscription records, was the anniversary of the Maundy: it was the only occasion upon which Edward VIII was to participate in the ceremony. At Westminster Abbey that morning he personally distributed the alms, a tradition which had lapsed after 1685 but which had been revived by his father. George V, in 1932 [*The Times*, 11th April, 1936, p. 9]. As far as the King and Mrs Simpson were concerned, however, the anniversary seems to refer to another, more private Eastertime event, it being at this moment in 1934 that the Prince bid his final adieus to his friend, Thelma, Viscountess Furness. [*Letters*, pp. 110-112]. Indeed, the latter's tactful exit might explain the earlier of the two inscriptions, 'eanum pig' perhaps being one of the Prince of Wales' fond names for his future wife.

124. AN EMERALD AND DIAMOND BRACELET
French, 1935

Designed as three step-cut emeralds with cut corners, each collet engraved with the weight: 6.59 carats, 8.14 carats and 6.29 carats respectively, alternating with three step-cut diamonds, and connected by sections of five baguette diamonds, *the tongue piece inscribed and dated: W – 25. XII 35 – D.*

Mrs Simpson and the Prince of Wales were obliged to spend Christmas, 1935, apart. She told her aunt that she and her husband, Ernest, 'have no Xmas plans [but] will of course be in London . . . I think Xmas an awful beating, everyone trying to be gay and eating too much and wondering how they'll pay for the presents they have given.' The Prince, enjoying the festive season no better, wrote to Mrs Simpson on Boxing Day from Sandringham, 'Good night and good morning my sweetheart . . . I couldn't believe it was possible to miss this way but its so lovely although hell while it lasts. It really is terrible here and so much the worst Xmas I've ever had to spend with the family, far worse than last year and that was bad enough . . . ' [*Letters*, pp. 165/6.]

125. AN EMERALD AND DIAMOND EARCLIP
mounted by Cartier

Designed as a flowerhead cluster, set at the centre with a square step-cut emerald with cut corners within a border of navette diamonds, *inscribed and numbered: Monture Cartier P. 9834.*

opposite, counter-clockwise from top: ills. 126, 127, 128 and 129.

126. A PAIR OF GOLD
AND EMERALD PENANNULAR BANGLES
probably circa 1940

Each of coronet design set with nine emerald beads.

127. A GOLD, EMERALD AND
DIAMOND DRESS RING
by Cartier, Paris, 1955

The front with five rows of emerald beads in a *bombé* cluster, the shoulders of diamond-set papyrus blossom motifs, the edges of the bezel *pavé*-set with brilliant-cut diamonds, *inscribed in the shank: Cartier, Paris; numbered: N 7584.*

The following weights are recorded in Cartier's archives: twenty-nine emerald beads: 49.96 carats; twenty-four diamonds: 1:62 carats.

128. A GOLD, RUBY AND DIAMOND DRESS RING
mounted by Cartier, Paris, 1963

The front designed as four rows of ruby beads, edged on each side of the bezel with brilliant-cut diamonds the shoulders and shank in a tapered fluted design, *signed and numbered: Monture Cartier P 8485.*

129. A PAIR OF GOLD,
EMERALD AND ROSE DIAMOND EARRINGS
mounted by Cartier, Paris, 1957

Each of foliate design set with rose diamonds and two bands of emeralds, *signed and numbered: Monture Cartier 9830.*

The following weight is recorded in Cartier's archives: twenty-two emerald beads: 42:17 carats.

Rubies

The name ruby, from the Latin *ruber* meaning 'red', described the red variety of the gem species *corundum*. The brilliant red colour of a fine ruby was as irresistible throughout history as it is today. As with many gemstones, the ruby was cherished not only for its beauty, but also for the many magical powers attributed to it. The stone inserted into the owner's flesh through a self-inflicted wound would confer invulnerability; good health, wisdom and success in love would also follow.

The world's most important source of gem-quality rubies has always been the Mogok area of Upper Burma, situated about ninety miles northeast of Mandalay. Here rubies are found principally in alluvial (riverbed) deposits weathered out of a crystalline limestone or marble. These mines were in operation well before 1597, when the King of Burma secured the territory from a local ruler. Native labourers, who were employed using primitive methods, were obliged by law to surrender all rubies over a certain weight and value to the King.

In 1886 the British annexed Burma and shortly afterwards, in 1889, the Burma Ruby mines Ltd., a London-based company and brainchild of E. W. Streeter, was floated to exploit the deposits by using modern techniques. Profits, however, were sporadic, and the enterprise went into voluntary liquidation in 1925. Thereafter the Mogok area reverted back to the native miners and their old methods.

Today the situation in Burma is a matter of conjecture. Since 1962, when the country's Socialist government took possession of the mines, reliable figures for ruby production have been impossible to obtain. Few foreigners are allowed to visit the area. Some say the mines are nearly depleted, and all agree that the demand for fine rubies far exceeds the supply. That this was always the case is evident from the statement made by the seventeenth-century French explorer and gem merchant Jean-Baptiste Tavernier: 'When a ruby exceeds 6 carats and is perfect, it is sold for whatever is asked for it.'

130. AN INVISIBLY SET RUBY AND DIAMOND CLIP
by Van Cleef & Arpels, Paris, 1936

Designed as two 'feuilles de houx', one set with *calibré-cut* rubies and baguette diamonds, the other with baguette and brilliant-cut diamonds, *signed: Van Cleef & Arpels; and inscribed: Breveté S.G.D.G. 45907.*

Van Cleef & Arpels' archives in Paris record that this jewel, one of the first with stones 'invisibly' set, was purchased by King Edward VIII in November, 1936. 'The two feathers,' he confirmed in a letter to Mrs Simpson of 1st January, 1937, 'were for *Christmas*' [*Letters*, p. 264]. (See also Sylvie Raulet, *Van Cleef & Arpels*, Paris, 1986, p. 207, a photograph of the Duchess of Windsor wearing the brooch in her hair: '. . . *dans ces cheveux un double clip "Feuilles de houx" en rubis sertis invisibles et diamants*'; and American *Vogue*, 1st December, 1941, p. 87.)

In the Spring of 1937, when Mrs Simpson was staying with Mr and Mrs Herman Rogers during her enforced separation from the Duke of Windsor at the Château de Candé, she received a visit from the photographer, Cecil Beaton. He was there representing the magazine *Vogue* for whom he was to take a number of studio portraits of her. He recalled of the session that, 'Jewellery was produced in unostentatious driblets. It impressed me to see some big historic stones, including a pair of diamond pear-shaped clips the size of pigeons' eggs.' The previous evening at dinner Beaton had observed of Mrs Simpson that she 'sported a new jewel in the form of two huge quills, one set with diamonds, the other with rubies.' [Cecil Beaton, *The Wandering Years Diaries: 1922-1939*, London, 1961, pp. 304 and 306.]

131. A PAIR OF INVISIBLY SET RUBY AND DIAMOND EARCLIPS
by Van Cleef & Arpels, New York

Each clip designed as an ivy leaf set with *calibré-cut* rubies and baguette diamonds, *signed and numbered: Van Cleef & Arpels N.Y. 12456.*

132. A RUBY AND DIAMOND NECKLACE
by Van Cleef & Arpels, 1939

Of *entrelac-de-rubans* design, the two ribbons set with baguette diamonds and cushion-shaped rubies respectively, the front supporting a detachable draped tassel set with similarly cut rubies and circular-cut diamonds, *inscribed and dated on one clasp: My Wallis from her David 19.VI.36; (sic) and signed and numbered on the other clasp: V.C.A. 236-CS.*

The inscription records Edward VIII's gift to Mrs Simpson on her fortieth birthday, 19th June, 1936. Van Cleef & Arpels in Paris have stated that Edward VIII purchased from them on 7th March, 1936, a ruby and diamond necklace, number 80246. The original design for the *festonné* chains is preserved in the firm's archives and the necklace itself is clearly visible in a photograph by Cecil Beaton of Mrs Simpson taken at the time. It was apparently redesigned in its present form by Renée-Sim Lacaze in 1939. The necklace seen here, which incorporates the original dedicatory inscription, was ordered from Van Cleef & Arpels by the Duke of Windsor in 1939 and delivered later the same year on the 20th of July. See Sylvie Raulet, *Van Cleef & Arpels*, Paris, 1986, p. 207.

*T*he Duke and Duchess of
Windsor photographed at a ball in the late 1930s. Note the
ruby and diamond clip by Van Cleef & Arpels (ill. 130).

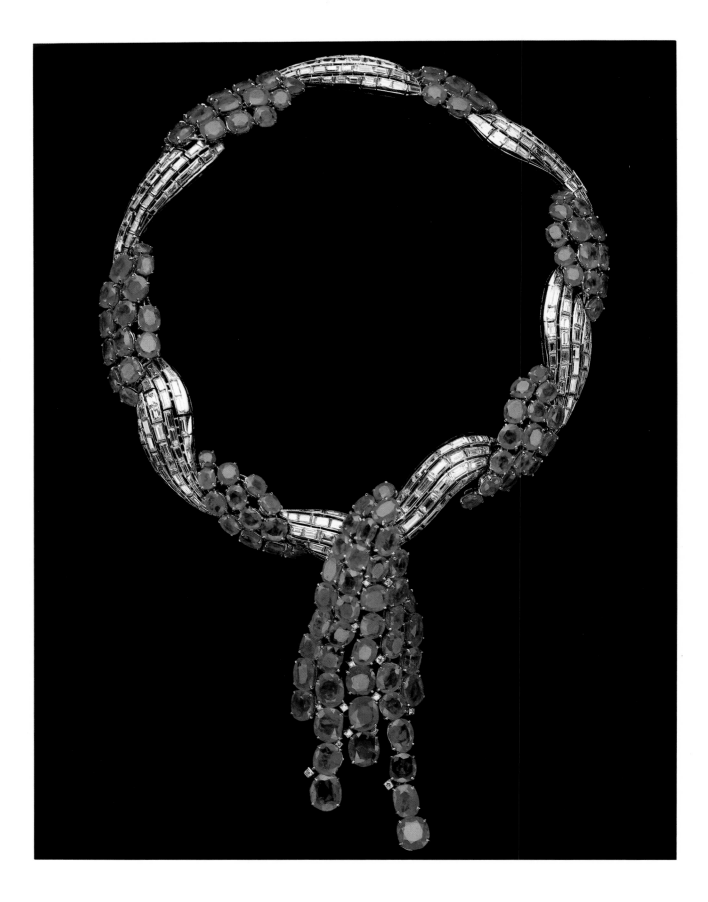

133-136. *Original designs for the ruby and diamond jewels seen in ills. 130 and 132, all from the Paris archives of Van Cleef & Arpels.*

Edward, Prince of Wales, succeeded to the throne as Edward VIII upon the death of his father on 20th January, 1936. It was not an easy time as Wallis Simpson, who in addition was worried about her health, told her Aunt Bessie in a letter at the end of the vacation: 'I have not got an ulcer but the type of stomach that needs care . . . I must take a house. I could not have remained in [Bryanston Court] under any conditions. It is too difficult for the King to come to flats and I have been advised by Duff Cooper etc that a house is necessary. . . . I have been here ten days for Ascot—which was not brilliant, having rained at some time every day and the same people. We had a nice party here.'

But there was much more on Mrs Simpson's mind at that moment besides her health and the weather. She confessed as much to her Aunt Bessie in a letter of 4th May, explaining for the first time that she had been attempting, with diminishing success, for over a year to maintain her position both as Ernest Simpson's wife as well as the favourite of the Prince of Wales who had now become King. 'It is hard I know for you to understand all that I am going to tell you,' she wrote, continuing, 'It is not easy to please, amuse, placate two men and to fit into two separate lives. . . . The result is I am tired, nervous and irritable to say nothing of the old nervous indigestion returning from time to time. . . . Divorce I am not planning at the moment. . . . The K on the other hand has [marriage] only in his mind. Whether I would allow such a drastic action depends on many things and events. . . . I have discussed all this with Ernest. Naturally he is sad but sees my point, he knows HM's devotion to me is deep and of the right sort. . . . I am sorry to have to tell you all this for I know you worry so much—but you see I am 40 and I feel I must follow my own instincts as regards my life and am quite prepared to pay for a mistake. . . .' [Letters, pp. 196-199.]

'Chips' Channon confided to his diary on 27th July,

1936, that, 'At Supper at Emerald [Cunard's], Mrs Simpson was literally smothered in rubies, and looking very well, as she has been on a fish diet for four days. Like me, she is worn out, but looks handsome, as I do, too.' An interesting comment from one who confessed to being 'rivetted by lust, furniture, glamour and society and jewels.' [Robert Rhodes James, editor, Chips The Diaries of Sir Henry Channon, London, 1967, pp. 38 and 73.]

opposite
137. A RUBY AND DIAMOND BRACELET
by Van Cleef & Arpels, Paris, 1936

In a design of four rectangular *bombé* links each set with ten cushion-shaped rubies between courses of baguette and circular-cut diamonds, alternating with smaller similarly shaped links set with baguette and circular-cut diamonds, *inscribed on the clasp: Hold Tight 27-iii-36; signed and numbered: Van Cleef & Arpels, Paris, 44430.*

Designed by René-Sim Lacaze and sold to King Edward VIII in March, 1936 [Van Cleef & Arpels' archives, Paris].

The King and Mrs Simpson spent the weekend of 27th March, 1936, with a few guests including her husband, Ernest, and their good friend, Mary Kirk Raffray, at the Fort. A few days later, the King wrote in the baby language he and Wallis Simpson reserved for their private correspondence, that 'THEY say that THEY liked this bracelet and that THEY want you to wear it always in the evening.' This was while the couple were staying, again with Mr Simpson and Mrs Raffray, at Lord Dudley's house, Himley Hall, Worcestershire. The letter concluded, 'THEY have told Mr Van Cleef but are very sad THEY can't make christen [sic] or write tonight. A boy loves a girl more and more and more.' [Letters, pp. 194, 321.] For further reference to the phrase 'Hold tight', see note to ill. 207.

The Duke and Duchess of Windsor at a New Year's Eve party in New York in 1949. Note the ruby and diamond necklace by Van Cleef & Arpels (ill. 132) and the ruby and diamond bangle (ill. 139).

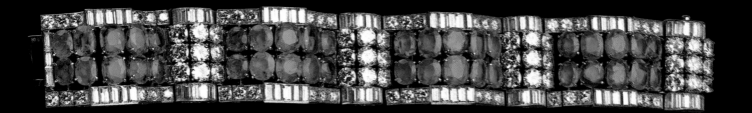

138. A PAIR OF RUBY AND DIAMOND EARCLIPS
mounted by Cartier, Paris, 1965

Each designed as a stylized flowerhead cluster, set with cushion-shaped rubies and baguette and circular-cut diamonds, *inscribed: Monture Cartier P 9870; one of the rubies has been replaced by a synthetic.*

The following weights are recorded in Cartier's archives: two oval rubies: 2.95 and 2.30 carats; eighteen oval rubies: 16.38 carats; sixty-four brilliant-cut diamonds: 4.45 carats; ninety-four baguette diamonds: 3.72 carats.

below
139. A RUBY AND DIAMOND HINGED PENNANNULAR BANGLE
by Cartier, Paris, 1938

The two large terminals at the front each set with a cushion-shaped ruby within a border of *pavé*-set brilliant-cut diamonds, the sides of the bezel similarly set with four rows of diamonds, the shoulders set with a tapered band of baguette diamonds, the back hinged and sprung, *the interior inscribed: For our first anniversary of June third; signed and numbered: Cartier, Paris, 04572.* The following weights are recorded in Cartier's archives: two cushion-shaped rubies: 36.15 carats; thirty baguette diamonds: 2.62 carats; brilliant-cut diamonds: 23 carats approximately.

The Duke and Duchess of Windsor's first wedding anniversary, 3rd June, 1938, appears to have been spent at La Croë, a villa at Antibes, the lease of which they had taken in the spring of that year. Harold Nicolson wrote to his wife from the South of France in August following a visit there. The Duke and Duchess, who were still dazed by the recent months of crisis, 'have a villa here and a yacht, and go round and round. He digs in the garden.' [Harold Nicolson, *Diaries and Letters, 1930-39*, London, 1966, p. 152.]

A photograph by Cecil Beaton of the Duchess of Windsor wearing the Cartier ruby and diamond bangle (ill. 139), and her emerald and diamond engagement ring (ill. 120).

A Jewel Box

Confiding to her diary early in 1937, Marie Belloc Lowndes recorded her surprise, expressed at a luncheon party, that, considering how simply Mrs Simpson dressed, the King's favourite "wore such a mass of dressmakers' jewels." At this, the other guests screamed with laughter because all her jewellery, they declared, was real! This delightful story is but one of many concerning the contents of the future Duchess of Windsor's jewel box. When in October 1946 intelligence reached Fleet Street of the Ednam Lodge robbery, in which the Duchess lost a number of pieces, journalists were not alone in becoming delirious in their speculations about the size of the haul. The Windsor collection was indeed magnificent and costly, but its wealth lay in its broad appeal, its several moods and colours, above all in the fact that many of its components were not originally of immense commercial value.

Coral was evidently one of the Duchess of Windsor's preferred materials, its warm pinkish-red tone having been sought for centuries by beautiful women. The type with which collectors of jewellery are most familiar is traditionally made from a tree-like species of the genus called *Corallium rubrum* found at its greatest perfection on the southern shores of the Mediterranean Sea. Coral became popular in the nineteenth century, when it was extensively used either in the natural twig form or, cut and polished or carved, in more sophisticated shapes for mounting in gold. More recently the use of coral was revived by Cartier in Paris to create a number of additions to their already extraordinary range of *objets d'art* and jewellery (ills. 157, 158, 159 and 161).

Jewels that employ both the amethyst and the turquoise were not entirely unknown before Cartier's introduced a collection in the late 1940's. The examples purchased by the Duchess of Windsor, perhaps the first to wear them, startled as much for the daring of their innovative designs as they did for the unusual juxtaposition of colours (ills. 162, 163, 164 and 165).

The name of the amethyst, from the Greek and originally so called because it was supposed to prevent intoxication, is applied to all the violet and purple crystals of quartz whose characteristic colour derives from the presence of oxide of manganese. Found in nearly all parts of the world, amethyst of the highest quality comes from Brazil, Uruguay and Siberia. The turquoise, or 'Turkish stone', a gem without transparency whose colour has been described poetically by E. W. Streeter as 'sky blue, out of a green, in which may be imagined a little milkish infusion,' is said to have been first discovered in Turkestan, although it was also extensively worked by the ancient Mexicans. These stones have since been found in many locations, such as Arizona, Nevada, California and Victoria.

The charm of the Duchess of Windsor's mid-1960's frog demi parure (ill. 178) and the shell earrings (ills. 174-177), while amusing in themselves, resides chiefly in the fact that they demonstrate her continued love of the whimsical in jewellery well into old age. Whereas the impact of her flamingo clip and 'great cat' pieces (ills. 140, 179, 181, 182, 185, 187 and 188) relies principally on highly original settings of diamonds and other gemstones, the frogs and shells, whose intrinsic value is by contrast small, are simply decorated. In one case the predominant colours are supplied by the use of brilliant green enamel and twirls of gold and in the other by the palette of nature itself arranged in a series of graceful spirals dotted with little gold chips. The Duchess' once considerable collection of costume jewellery included other examples in this taste, while one of her most fantastic possessions was a gold evening purse made in the shape of an adored pug dog.

140. A RUBY, SAPPHIRE, EMERALD, CITRINE AND DIAMOND CLIP
mounted by Cartier, Paris, 1940

Designed as a flamingo in characteristic pose, the plumage set with *calibré*-cut emeralds, rubies and sapphires, the beak set with a cabochon citrine and sapphire, the eye set with a similarly cut sapphire, the head, neck, body and legs *pavé*-set with brilliant-cut diamonds, the legs hinged, *signed on the clasp: MONTURE Cartier, and numbered: L 5730.*

Created by Jeanne Toussaint for Cartier's; for further comment, see Suzy Menkes, *The Royal Jewels*, London, 1986, chapter 4, and p. 79.

The Duchess of Windsor is known to have worn this brooch soon after acquiring it when she and the Duke arrived at the Ritz Hotel, Madrid, on his forty-sixth birthday, 23rd June, 1940 [Michael Bloch, *Operation Willi*, London, 1984, 2nd p. of photographs after p. 82].

141. A PLATINUM POCKET PHOTOGRAPH FRAME
by Cartier, London, 1947

Oval form, the front engraved with the cypher of the Duchess of Windsor, *the interior inscribed: All the things I said each year in the other locket 1935-1946 1947—More & more & more Wallis from David Easter 1947; signed; Cartier, London;* containing a coloured photograph of the Duke and Duchess of Windsor.

The phrase 'more and more' is one frequently used by the Duke of Windsor in his love letters to Mrs Simpson, particularly during the distressing time prior to their reunion and marriage at Candé in 1937. His message to her from Landhaus Appesbach on 14th April that year is typical: 'Oh! my beloved one . . . . This is just a line to say I love you more and more my own sweetheart and praying that the next eighteen days and nights won't drag too interminably for WE [Wallis and Edward]. Poor WE—and there must be a huge store of happiness for us after all these months of hell. . . . ' [*Letters*, p. 309]. See ills. 94 (9) and 125.

142. A 14 CARAT GOLD LOCKET
by Cartier, circa 1948

Circular, the front with St. Christopher and the words: ST-CHRISTOPHER LOOK AT ME AND BE SAFE, the interior with two compartments, *the reverse inscribed and dated: From* MARGARET B PALM BEACH FEB 29, 1948, *signed: Cartier.*

Margaret Biddle, a friend of the Windsors, was the wife of Anthony Drexel Biddle Jr. (1896–1961), U.S. Ambassador to Poland immediately prior to the Second World War, whom the Duchess of Windsor had met years before in Baltimore during his bachelor days. He and the Duchess renewed their acquaintanceship aboard S.S. *Excalibur* in the Summer of 1940 when he was on his way back to Washington and she and the Duke were about to take up their residence in Nassau [*The Heart Has Its Reasons*, London, 1956, p. 344; *Vogue*, American edition, 1st March, 1943, pp. 76/7.]

143. AN EMERALD, RUBY AND DIAMOND BROOCH
by Cartier, Paris, 1930's

Designed as a 20-peso gold coin, 1918, within a border of brilliant-cut diamonds, and *calibré*-cut rubies and emeralds, on a similarly set scroll brooch hanger; *signed: Cartier.*

144. A THREE-COLOURED GOLD AND RUBY CIRCULAR PENDANT
probably circa 1940

Designed as a tropical seascape, a palm tree in the foreground, the ruby sun setting on the horizon, a sailing vessel in the distance.

145. A 14 CARAT GOLD, EMERALD AND DIAMOND PENDANT
circa 1937

The circular medallion applied at the centre with a carved emerald and diamond representation of the Indian deity Ganesch and a lady's diamond slipper, *the reverse inscribed and dated: "Our Mr Loo" 7.VII.34 6.IV.37.*

The applied slipper on this medallion refers to the cairn terrier of that name, alias 'Mr. Loo,' who was born on 7th July, 1934, and given to Mrs Simpson by the Prince of Wales as a Christmas present the same year. The presence of the Indian deity Ganesch is surely a reference to the sadness, but with hopes of diminished sorrow in the future, which Slipper's untimely death caused at an already critical moment in the lover's relationship. Considering how fond the couple were to become of the little dog and how distraught they were at his passing, this modest jewel is perhaps the most touching item in the Duchess's collection. For a photograph of her with Slipper ['Mr Loo'], see *Letters*.

The Duchess of Windsor later recalled that, 'Part of my affection for the Fort extended to the Prince's cairns, Cora and Jaggs. When the men were off golfing, I often took them with me for a walk through the grounds, and we became good friends. Unknown to me the Prince had observed the growth of our friendship. One afternoon he turned up a Bryanston Court with a cairn puppy under his arm. "This," he said, "is Slipper. He is yours." Aunt Bessie Merryman learnt of Slipper in a letter written by Mrs Simpson from Fort Belvedere on 3rd December, 1934: 'I have a cairn puppy—adorable and aged 4 1/2 months. You will love him,' adding, 'I have 2 more bracelets and a small diamond that sticks into my hair. Smart. Ernest says the insurance is getting steep!'

During the difficult period immediately prior to Edward VIII's renunciation of his rights to the throne, finalized on 10th December, 1936, Mrs Simpson fled to France (see ill. 114), leaving Slipper behind. The dog remained, an emotional link between the lovers, until the King, now Duke of Windsor, arranged for him to be sent to Mrs Simpson at Candé. The Duchess later remembered the 'dog's joyous recognition [of me] was like a signal . . . that, along with Slipper, David had sent part of himself.' The Duke wrote an accompanying letter on 22nd March, 1937, from Schloss Enzesfeld, where he was then staying, saying, 'Sweetheart Here is Mr. Loo and a few eanum things I'm sending you . . . Oh! Wallis I love you so and please take enormous care . . . Slipper will give you a dog kiss from your own David.'

The dog arrived at Candé on 24th March. A few days later on 6th April, however, a terrible thing happened while Mrs Simpson and friends were playing golf, Slipper and a pair of Scotties tagging along. 'Slipper and the Scotties,' wrote the Duchess, 'suddenly tore off into the woods in pursuit of a rabbit. The Scotties reappeared, but Slipper was missing . . . I became worried . . . [We then] started back through the woods to look for him. As we emerged near the first green, I saw what seemed to be a grey rag on the grass. It was Slipper . . . When I tried to come near he raised himself as in a spasm. I had a dreadful time picking him up. He twisted and tried to bite me. There was no mistaking what had happened to Slipper. In his foray into the undergrowth he had run afoul of a viper . . . Slipper died early that evening at the veterinary's in Tours . . . His loss on the eve of my reunion with David seemed to me a frightful omen. He had been our companion in joy and trouble; now he was gone. Was everything that I loved to be destroyed?' On the day after the little dog's death, Mrs Simpson wrote two grief-stricken letters,

one to Mrs Merryman, the other to her fiancé. In his, the equally distressed Duke read, ' . . . He was our dog— not yours or mine but ours—and he loved us both so. Now the principal guest at the Wedding is no more. I can't stop crying . . . ' [*Letters*, pp. 124, 298/9, 301, 305/6; *The Heart Has Its Reasons*, pp. 194/5, 294.]

146. A GOLD AND DIAMOND BROOCH
by Cartier, Paris, late 1930's

The circular medallion of the Holy Virgin with the legend: *N.S.D. GUADALUPE DE MEXICO. A. 1804* the reverse with the legend: *NON FECIT TALITER OMNINATIONI*, mounted within a border of brilliant-cut diamonds and suspended from a diamond-set scroll brooch hanger; *signed: Cartier.*

173

175

147. AN 18 CARAT GOLD AND GEM-SET BIB NECKLACE
by Cartier, Paris, 1945

The front composed of lozenge-shaped motifs in a draped articulated design set with cabochon and step-cut rubies and emeralds and brilliant-cut diamonds, *marked and numbered on the clasp: M 5174.*

The following weights are recorded in Cartier's archives: one hundred and thirty-eight diamonds: 7.63 carats; forty-nine rubies: 49.11 carats; forty emeralds: 35.01 carats.

Suzy Menkes has written: 'This dramatic lattice necklace studded with rubies and emeralds was made by Cartier in October 1945 by breaking up two gem-set brooches, two pairs of earrings and an emerald ring.' [*The Royal Jewels*, London, 1986, p. 95.]

148. AN 18 CARAT GOLD, SAPPHIRE, RUBY AND DIAMOND HINGED BANGLE
by Cartier, Paris, 1946

The front designed as a peacock's feather, the centre set with a course of baguette diamonds between carved sapphires and brilliant-cut diamonds, the tips of the feather set with radiating rows of ruby beads, each set with a diamond, the eye of the feather forming the clasp and set with a large carved sapphire representing a female profile within a foliate border, the back decorated with three rows of corded wire, *signed and numbered: Cartier, Paris 5531.* The following weights are recorded in Cartier's archives: one engraved sapphire: 28.77 carats; eighty-one ruby beads: 40.20 carats (including the missing stone); seventeen carved sapphires: 17.60 carats; ninety-seven brilliant-cut diamonds: 2.30 carats; twenty-four baguette diamonds: 4.62 carats.

149. A MASSIVE PARCEL-GILT SILVER PENANNULAR BANGLE
by Cartier, circa 1940

Of North African inspiration, decorated with three rows of gilt beads flanked by stepped and fluted borders, *the interior inscribed: For a happier New Year NASSAU 1-1-41 WE; signed: Cartier.*

The difficulties experienced by the Duke and Duchess of Windsor during 1939 and '40 were described by her in *The Heart Has Its Reasons*, chapters 30, 31 and 32. At the close of this unsettled time, the Duke was offered, and accepted, the post of Governor and Commander-in-Chief of the Bahamas during 1940, sailing on 1st August from Lisbon via Bermuda to Nassau. He and the Duchess remained there, except for brief excursions, until the end of the War.

As a well-known, successful hostess, the Duchess was invited at this time to share her opinions on entertaining with the readers of American *Vogue*. She wrote that the 'flowers and table decorations at Government House [Nassau] are done by me . . . We use for the table mainly native fruits, the lovely papaya, the breadfruit . . . Since all our silver was left behind in France, I use glass on the table . . . ' Regarding dress on the island, her philosophy, 'as everywhere, is simply to look neat, appropriate, and inconspicuous . . . (Never the sensational dress) . . . I don't give much time to clothes, as mine are just correct, well-cut, and of good materials, allowing me to wear them for several years . . . Since I can't be pretty, I try to look sophisticated . . . ' [Wallis Windsor, "Jotted Down", *Vogue*, American edition, 15th July, 1943, pp. 26/27/74]. See photograph on p. 174.

A*photograph by Horst*
taken in the 1940s of the Duchess of Windsor wearing the bib necklace (ill. 147).
opposite
149. *From Cartier's Paris archives, a designer's drawing for the jewelled bangle seen in ill. 148.*

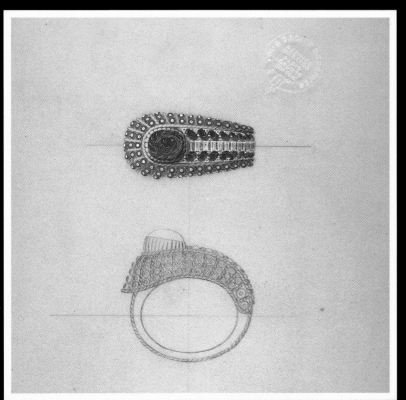

opposite, clockwise from top center: ills. 150, 151, 153 and 152.

150. A GOLD, RUBY AND SAPPHIRE CLIP
by Cartier, Paris, 1946

Designed as a stylised spray composed of *festonné* chains of ruby and sapphire beads supported by rondels of corded wire and chains of plaited gold, *signed: Cartier, Paris.*

151. A PAIR OF 18 CARAT WHITE GOLD, SAPPHIRE AND DIAMOND EARCLIPS
by Cartier, Paris, circa 1950

Designed as a circle of diamonds supporting four hoops of sapphire beads, the two larger hoops at the centre, *signed: Cartier, Paris, number illegible.*

152. A PAIR OF 18 CARAT GOLD AND SAPPHIRE EARCLIPS
by Cartier, Paris, 1949

Each designed as a wide tapered hoop pierced in a lattice and supporting a fringe of sapphire beads, each capped by blue glass beads, *signed and numbered on the clasps; Cartier, 01477.*

153. A PAIR OF 18 CARAT GOLD, RUBY AND DIAMOND EARCLIPS
mounted by Cartier, Paris, circa 1950

Each of stylised creole design, the oval centre set with three rose diamonds and supporting three hoops of ruby beads, the largest at the centre, *signed and numbered: monture, Cartier P 8484.*

below
154. A SILVER PHOTOGRAPH FRAME
maker's mark rubbed, London, 1910

Rectangular, the silver cagework mount enclosing panels of stained blue hardstone, height 9 cm., width 6 cm., easel support. Containing a later informal black and white photograph of the Duke and Duchess of Windsor bathing in the sea.

155. A GOLD, TURQUOISE,
AMETHYST AND DIAMOND
BIB NECKLACE
by Cartier, Paris, 1947

The front of lattice design set with step-cut amethysts, brilliant-cut diamonds, and turquoises, with a larger heart-shaped amethyst at the front surmounted by three baguette diamonds, on a chain of Prince of Wales linking, *signed on the clasp: Cartier France.*

The following weights are recorded in Cartier's archives: twenty-nine amethysts: 158.9 carats; twenty-three baguette diamonds: 1.82 carats; one-hundred and eighty-eight brilliant-cut diamonds: 8.84 carats; two-hundred turquoises: 33.65 carats.

overleaf The Duchess of Windsor
*wearing the amethyst and turquoise necklace
(ill. 155) at the Gala Ball, Versailles, in June, 1953.*

156. *Designer's drawing, from the Paris archives of
Cartier, for the necklace seen in ill. 155.*

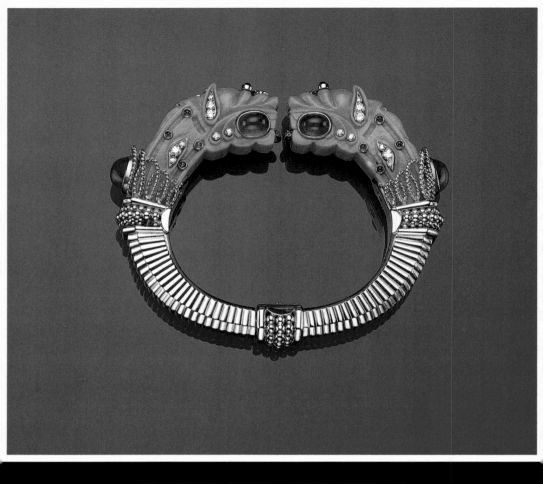

overleaf
157. AN 18 CARAT GOLD, CORAL, EMERALD AND DIAMOND CHOKER
by Cartier, Paris, 1949

Designed as a skein of twenty-four rows of coral beads, on a tubular clasp, set with carved emerald foliate motifs and eight-cut diamonds, the centre set with a row of brilliant-cut diamonds, *the clasp signed: Cartier, Paris.* The following weights are recorded in Cartier's archives: Sixteen carved emeralds: 12.07 carats. Fifty diamonds: 1.67 carats.

opposite above
158. AN 18 CARAT GOLD, CORAL, EMERALD AND DIAMOND HINGED BANGLE
by Cartier, Paris, 1947

The front with two corals carved as confronted dragons' heads, each set with cabochon emeralds and eight-cut diamonds, their necks decorated with corded wire and set with cabochon emeralds, with swivel action hinge, *signed: Cartier, Paris, and numbered indistinctly: 06660.*

opposite below
159. AN 18 CARAT GOLD, CORAL, EMERALD AND DIAMOND CLIP
by Cartier, Paris, 1946

Designed as a butterfly, set with a step-cut emerald and baguette- and eight-cut diamonds, perched on a flowerhead set with a large cabochon coral and step-cut emeralds, the stalk set with diamonds, *signed and numbered: Cartier, Paris, 09533.*

The following weights are recorded in Cartier's archives: eight emeralds: 1.97 carats; sixty-three diamonds: 0.91 carats. See ill. 161 for a ring of complementary design.

*O*riginal drawing, from the Paris archives of Cartier, for the coral and gem-set ring seen below (ill. 161).

161. A GOLD AND GEM-SET RING
by Cartier, Paris, 1947

The bezel set with a cabochon coral within a gold border of leaf motifs set with step-cut emeralds and circular-cut diamonds, on a reeded gold shank, *signed: Cartier, France, and numbered: M 6730.* The following weights are recorded in Cartier's archives: ten emeralds: 1.58 carats; ten diamonds: 0.17 carat.

This ring is of complementary design to the brooch in ill. 159.

162. AN 18 CARAT GOLD, TURQUOISE AND SAPPHIRE DRESS RING
by Cartier, Paris, circa 1950

Of turban design, one side of the bezel *pavé*-set with five tapered rows of cushion-shaped sapphires, the other similarly set with turquoises, *signed and numbered: Cartier, Paris, 5918.*

163. AN 18 CARAT GOLD, AMETHYST, TURQUOISE AND DIAMOND LAPEL BROOCH
by Cartier, Paris, 1950

The terminal of conical form, the oval amethyst claw-set at the top within a double row border of brilliant-cut diamonds, the sides in a lattice design set with turquoises, the base *pavé*-set with brilliant-cut diamonds, connected to the two pins by a foliate motif set with baguette and brilliant-cut diamonds and turquoises, the

hinged pins capped by turquoise and diamond bud motifs, *signed and numbered: Cartier, Paris 010628.*

The following weights are recorded in Cartier's archives: amethyst: 30.30 carats; diamonds: 5.61 carats.

164. A PAIR OF 18 CARAT GOLD, AMETHYST, TURQUOISE AND DIAMOND EARCLIPS
by Cartier, Paris, 1947

Each designed as a stylised scroll motif set with a cluster of turquoises and a band of pear-shaped amethysts tipped by baguette and brilliant-cut diamond fleur-de-lys motifs, *signed: Cartier, FRANCE, numbered indistinctly: 6729.*

165. AN 18 CARAT GOLD, AMETHYST AND TURQUOISE CLIP
by Cartier, Paris, circa 1950

Designed as a heart, the similarly shaped amethyst mounted within a border of turquoises, *signed and numbered: Cartier, Paris, 011950.*

below

166. AN 18 CARAT GOLD AND DIAMOND NÉCESSAIRE DU SOIR
by Cartier, Paris, 1947

Tonneau-shaped, decorated in a reeded design and applied with diamond butterfly and flowerhead motifs, *the interior inscribed and dated: Wallis from Edward 1947; signed: Cartier FRANCE.*

This may have been a 10th wedding anniversary gift from the Duke of Windsor to his Duchess.

overleaf

167. A TWO-COLOURED GOLD ENAMEL, CULTURED PEARL, TOURMALINE AND QUARTZ NECKLACE
French, circa 1950

Designed as an articulated garland of leaves and flowers, the flowerheads set with variously-cut citrines, smoky quartz tourmalines and *mabé* pearls, the stems decorated with black enamel, *maker's poinçon two fishes between V and J.*

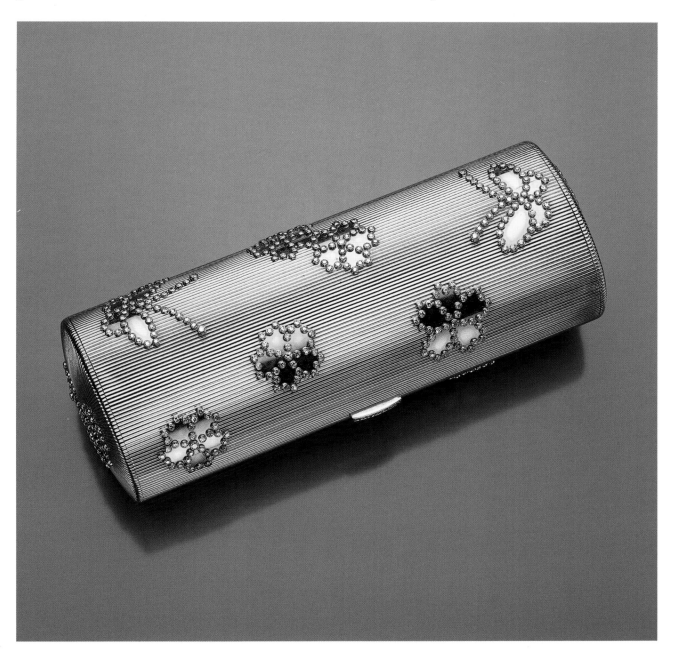

The Duchess of Windsor at a reception in Paris in 1970. Note the necklace (ill. 167).

168. A LADY'S 18 CARAT GOLD HANDBAG SUITE
by Van Cleef & Arpels, circa 1950

Comprising: a powder Compact, of basket weave design, the front applied with the Prince of Wales' feathers set with rose diamonds and emeralds and a ruby, *numbered: 50060*; a Pill Box, the front applied with the figure of a boy and girl set with a *calibré*-cut ruby and sapphire, a trapeze-shaped emerald and rose and brilliant-cut diamonds, *the interior inscribed: Peck, and numbered: 66046*; a Scent Bottle, prism-shaped, the top applied with the anchor of the Royal Navy, decorated with enamel and set with rose diamonds, *numbered: 50079*; a Lipstick Holder, of similar form, the top applied with an anchor, *numbered: 50076*; a Comb Case, the front applied with a horseshoe, the monogram of King George V and Queen Mary, and the cypher of Kaiser Wilhelm II, all gem-set, *numbered: 50077*; and

a Notebook Holder, applied with five motifs, comprising: an enamel and rose diamond horse and jockey, an enamel and rose diamond briar rose, a seed pearl and rose diamond ship's wheel, a crowned Irish Harp, and a medallion of King George V and Queen Mary within a border of rose diamonds, *numbered: 50076*, fitted with a notebook, *printed with the Duchess of Windsor's cypher; all pieces signed: Van Cleef & Arpels, and all, except the pill box, inscribed H. G. [sic] THE DUCHESS OF WINDSOR.*

169. AN 18 CARAT GOLD
AND DIAMOND EVENING BAG
by Van Cleef & Arpels, Paris, circa 1950

In a basket-weave design, the scalloped clasp *pavé*-set with brilliant- and eight-cut diamonds, the interior with a mirror, *signed and numbered: Van Cleef & Arpels 79797.*

170. A GOLD AND DIAMOND POWDER CASE
by Cartier, Paris, circa 1950

Designed as an egg with ropework borders, the front engraved with the royal arms as borne by the Duke of Windsor, the reverse with the initials WW in monogram for Wallis Windsor below a royal coronet, the thumbpiece set with a rose diamond, the pendant ring *pavé*-set with brilliant-cut diamonds, *signed: 'Cartier Paris', fitted case by Cartier.*

171. A 14 CARAT GOLD AND AQUAMARINE COMPACT
by Verdura, circa 1950

Of lobed heart-shaped design, the cover set with a large cabochon aquamarine, *signed: Verdura; 163 gms all in.*

The eccentric Sicilian aristocrat and designer of jewellery, Fulco Santostefano della Cerda, Duke of Verdura, Marquess of Murata la Cerda, more usually known simply as Verdura, came from an equally eccentric family; it is said that one of his ancestors fired a pistol at a nun for ruining the tranquility one afternoon by sounding the angelus too enthusiastically. Verdura himself, having spent his father's fortune on a fancy dress party soon after the latter's death, left Italy at the age of twenty-eight. He then went to Paris where he found employment as a textile designer with Coco Chanel. Afterwards the Duke went on to produce a range of personal ornaments for Chanel which, so different from the accepted type of fashionable jewellery with its reliance on large or valuable gems, mixed enamel, gold, precious and semi-precious stones in unusual, and sometimes startling, settings.

In 1937 Verdura transferred to New York where, after a brief employment with a jeweller later apprehended for the misuse of his client's property, he opened his own business on Fifth Avenue. He became well known in society as much for his wonderful bijoux as for his wit, wisdom and fund of amusing gossip. After the War, while maintaining his establishment in America, the Duke returned to Paris to sell jewellery from a new gallery. He retired in 1973 to London, where he had a flat in Eaton Square. He died aged 80 in 1978.

172. A GOLD MESH, RUBY TURQUOISE AND DIAMOND PURSE
by Van Cleef & Arpels, New York, 1942

The circular hinged cover set at the centre with a ruby and diamond flowerhead motif, within a border of turquoises, opening to reveal a wide expandable top to the purse, *signed and numbered indistinctly: Van Cleef & Arpels N.Y. 3320.*

According to the archives of Van Cleef & Arpels, New York, this purse, numbered 3320, was made in 1942 and purchased the following year by Mrs James Donahue.

Mrs James Donahue (1886–1971), an intimate of the Duchess of Windsor, was the former Jessie Woolworth and last surviving daughter of F. W. Woolworth, founder of the well-known chain store of that name. Her son, James ('Jimmy') Donahue (1915–1966), also a friend, became the constant companion of the Duke and Duchess from 1950 until 1954.

Being a great patron of Van Cleef & Arpels in Paris, Mrs Donahue was instrumental in the firm establishing a branch in New York. Those of her items from the latter to be found in the Duchess of Windsor's collection (this and ills. 112 and 172) were all purchased in November or December of the year specified; it is therefore assumed that they were Christmas presents to the Duchess either from Mrs Donahue or her son.

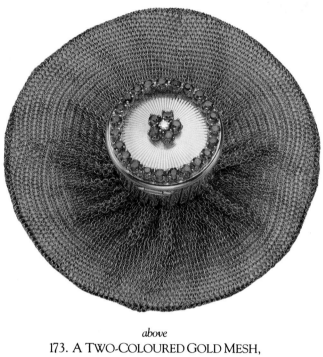

above

173. A TWO-COLOURED GOLD MESH, SAPPHIRE AND DIAMOND PURSE
by Van Cleef & Arpels, New York, 1954

The circular hinged cover decorated with a radiated motif and set at the centre with a sapphire and diamond cluster within a sapphire border, opening to reveal a wide expandable top to the purse, *signed and numbered: Van Cleef & Arpels N.Y. 22663.*

According to the archives of Van Cleef & Arpels, New York, this purse, numbered 22663, was made in 1954 and purchased the following year.

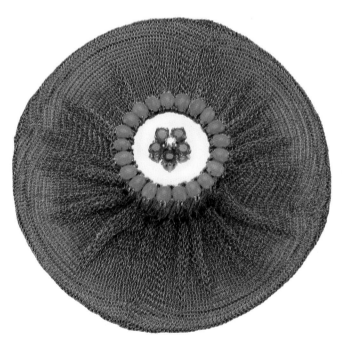

174. A PAIR OF 18 CARAT GOLD AND SHELL EARCLIPS
by David Webb, New York, 1964/65

Each designed as a brown, white and yellow striped shell (polymita picta, Cuban tree snails) applied with gold lozenge motifs, *signed on the clips: David Webb©.*

According to his firm, this and the following two

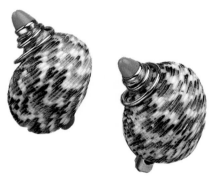

pairs of gold mounted shell earclips by David Webb were acquired by the Duchess of Windsor in 1964 and 1965. The first pair, from shells supplied by the Duchess herself, were made to an order received in May, 1965, just two months after the Duke had bought Webb's frog bracelet. The third and final pair of clips were mounted for the Duchess in January, 1965.

175. A PAIR OF GOLD, SHELL AND CORAL EARCLIPS
circa 1965

Each shell (probably turbinid) enclosed in a gold tendril capped with a coral cabochon, *unmarked.*

176. A PAIR OF 18 CARAT GOLD AND SHELL EARCLIPS
by David Webb, New York, 1964/65

Each designed as an orange, brown and white striped shell (polymita picta, Cuban tree snails) applied with gold lozenge motifs, *signed on the clips: David Webb©.*

177. A PAIR OF GOLD, SHELL AND TURQUOISE EARCLIPS
circa 1965

Each with a mottled shell in grey and white (neritina versicolour), capped with a gold and turquoise tendril, *unmarked.*

opposite
178. A GOLD, ENAMEL, RUBY AND DIAMOND DEMI PARURE
by David Webb, New York, 1964

Comprising: a bangle in a design of two confronted frogs, entirely decorated with bright green enamel applied with gold spiral motifs, the eyes set with cabochon rubies, the mouths with circular-cut diamonds; and a pair of earclips *en suite, signed: David Webb; enamel slightly imperfect.*

According to the firm of David Webb, the Duke of Windsor visited their New York shop in March 1964, and purchased the frog bracelet as a surprise gift for the Duchess. It is understood from the same source that the frog earclips were probably a gift to the Duchess from David Webb himself, who is known to have presented her with several presents of this nature. For reference to frogs, see ill. 94 (10).

Cats

Wallis Windsor's fascination with denizens of the natural world, while confined in the flesh to beloved Cairns and pug dogs, found expression in decorative motifs scattered throughout her scheme of fashion. The dresses of her 1936 trousseau, for instance, were stitched and appliquéd with a variety of creatures: yellow butterflies flitting against a pale-blue ground and little white turtles reposing in a sea of black crepe.

The Duchess' exotic flamingo clip, which the Duke probably gave her as a birthday gift on 19th June 1940, was the original of her important jewels in this taste (ill. 140). After the Ednam Lodge robbery of 1946, when thieves absconded with an amazing bird-of-paradise brooch then recently made up by Cartier from sapphires and diamonds unset from other pieces, the Duchess acquired the first of her panthers, a spotted gold and black enamel beast aroused from its slumber on a vast cabochon emerald. This proved to be the initial example in a celebrated series of 'great cat' jewels created by Cartier (ills. 179, 181, 182, 185, 186 and 188).

The inspiration for these jewels had come from Jeanne Toussaint (1887-1978), whose association with the firm began in 1915. An intimate companion of Louis Cartier (1874-1942), who affectionately named her 'Panther', Mme Toussaint indulged her own passion for the animal by scattering her apartment in Paris with panther skins. Further, she obtained from Cartier, around 1917, an onyx panther vanity case and, a little later, a black and gold striped compact and cigarette case, both mounted with onyx and diamond panthers. In 1934 Louis Cartier made her responsible for the *Haute-Joaillerie* of the firm, and soon afterwards she began conferring with the Duke and Duchess of Windsor on many jewel projects. The collaboration between Jeanne Toussaint and the firm's designers, most notably perhaps Peter Lemarchand (1906-1970), continued to blossom after the Second World War with the appearance of the life-like panther and tiger jewels, which became such a feature of the Windsor collection.

and six sapphires: 5 carats; brilliant-cut diamonds: 4:90 carats.

opposite below
180. AN 18 CARAT GOLD, ENAMEL AND DIAMOND CLIP
Italian, circa 1960

Designed as a panther, the muzzle *pavé*-set with eight-cut diamonds, the nose, tongue and ears decorated with red enamel, the body with black enamel spots.

opposite overleaf, left to right: ills. 181 (detail on facing page) and 182.
181. AN ONYX AND DIAMOND PANTHER BRACELET
by Cartier, Paris, 1952

The attenuated and articulated body designed to encircle the wrist and to assume a stalking attitude, *pavé*-set throughout with circular-cut diamonds and *calibré*-cut onyx, the eyes set with marquise-shaped emeralds, *the bracelet divides under the head and in the centre of the back, the tongue-piece of the latter inscribed: Cartier, Paris; the clasp numbered: 07532; several small stones deficient.*

182. AN ONYX AND DIAMOND PANTHER CLIP
by Cartier, Paris, 1966

The articulated animal in repose, the forepaws and tail extended, the head turned slightly to the right, *pavé*-set throughout with circular-cut diamonds and *calibré*-cut onyx, the eyes with pear-shaped emeralds, *signed and numbered on the clip: Cartier, Paris, 01875; one onyx deficient.*

opposite part-title page
179. A SAPPHIRE AND DIAMOND PANTHER CLIP
by Cartier, Paris, 1949

The panther *pavé*-set with diamonds and *calibré*-cut sapphire spots and with pear-shaped yellow diamond eyes, crouched on a large cabochon sapphire, *signed and numbered: Cartier Paris, 010166, one stone deficient.*

The following weights are recorded in Cartier's archives: cabochon sapphire: 152:35 carats; one hundred

above: 183. Designer's drawing, from the Paris archives of Cartier, for the jeweled panther clip seen in ill. 179.

The Duke and Duchess of Windsor leaving Claridge's Hotel, London, on 7th June, 1967, to attend the unveiling by Her Majesty the Queen of a memorial plaque to Queen Mary at Marlborough House. Note the sapphire panther clip (ill. 179).

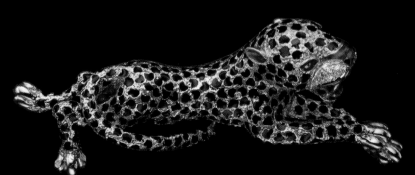

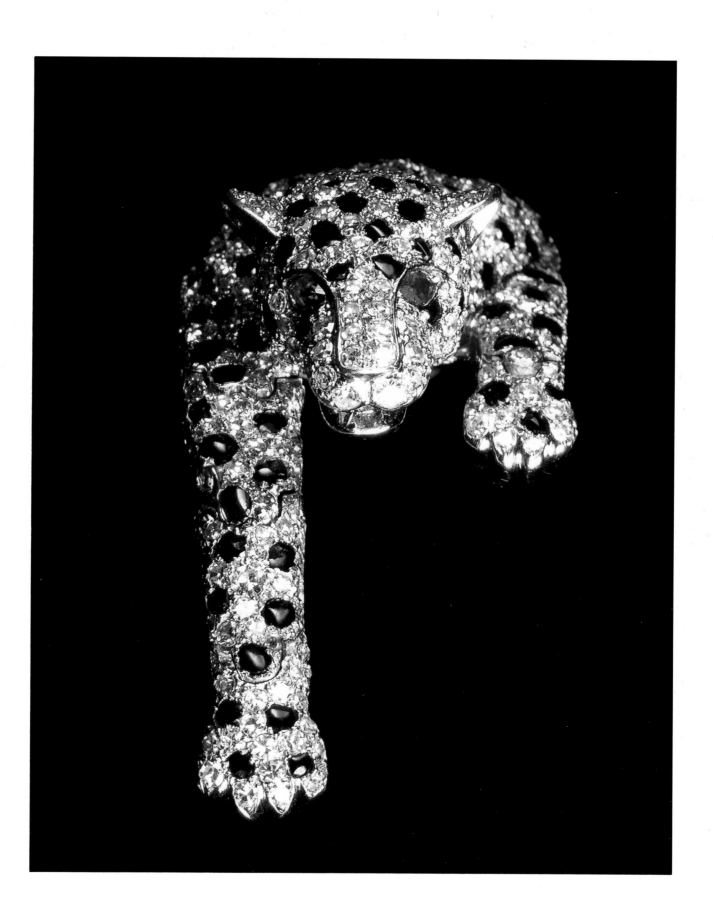

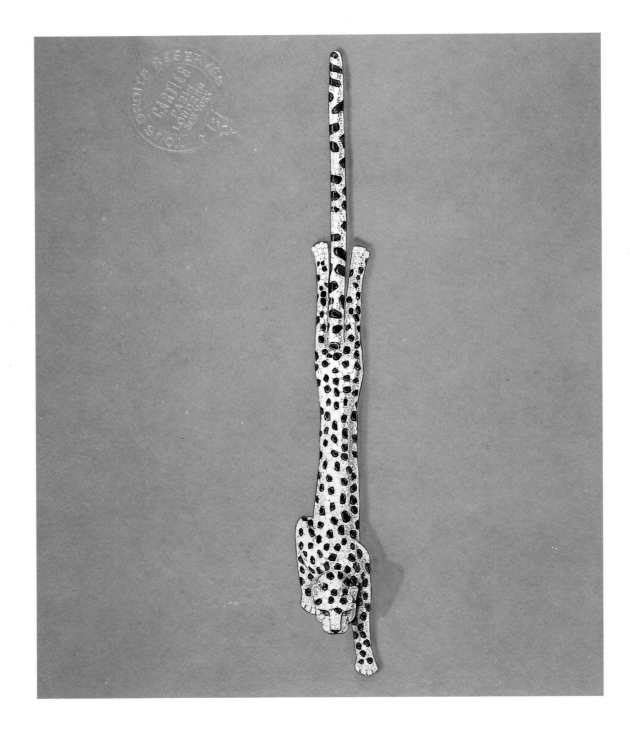

184. From Cartier's Paris archives,
the original design for the onyx and diamond panther
bracelet seen in ill. 181.

185. AN ONYX AND DIAMOND TIGER CLIP
by Cartier, Paris, 1959

The articulated animal in repose, the forepaws and tail extended, the tail and head articulated, *pavé*-set throughout with yellow circular-cut diamonds, the eyes with pear-shaped emeralds, *signed and numbered on the clasp: Cartier, Paris, R 2756.*

186. AN ONYX AND DIAMOND TIGER BRACELET
by Cartier, Paris, 1956

The attenuated and articulated body designed to en-circle the wrist, the legs hanging freely, *pavé*-set throughout with circular-cut yellow diamonds shading naturalistically in places to white, and bands of *calibré*-cut onyx, the eyes with marquise-shaped emeralds, *the bracelet divides under the head and in the centre of the back, signed on the latter tongue-piece: Cartier, Paris; and numbered on the clasp: N 8966.*

below
187. A GOLD, ENAMEL AND EMERALD PANTHER CLIP
by Cartier, Paris, 1948

The gold panther decorated with black enamel and with pear-shaped emerald eyes, crouched on a large cabochon emerald weighing approximately 90 carats, *signed: Cartier Paris.*

In his chapter on Cartier's 'great cat' jewels, Hans Nadelhoffer [*Cartier*, p. 230] has stated that this clip with its 'outstretched golden panther flecked with black. . . was the firm's first fully three-dimensional treatment of the motif.'

*O*n 11th December, 1959,
the Duchess of Windsor attended the gala opening of The Lido in Paris. This photograph, taken on that occasion, shows her wearing several items of jewellery including the panther bangle and clip (ills. 181 and 182), the tiger bracelet (ill. 186), and the "McLean" diamond (ill. 214).

opposite
188. AN 18 CARAT GOLD AND ENAMEL LORGNETTE
by Cartier, Paris, 1954

Designed as a tiger with a raised paw, decorated with black *champlevé* enamel, the eyes set with pear-shaped emeralds, *signed: Cartier, Paris, numbered indistinctly: 6882; enamel slightly imperfect; in a brocade pochette inscribed: Please return to HRH The Duchess of Windsor Reward.*

'The lorgnette has returned to fashion. The Duchess of Windsor . . . is especially fond of a pair which springs out from a small tiger handle of gold, striped in black enamel, emerald-eyed. Cartier in Paris designed it for her.' [*Vogue*, American edition, 1st May, 1955, p. 122, with a drawing by René Bouché of the Duchess holding the tiger lorgnette. See illustration.]

Suzy Menkes [*The Royal Jewels*, pp. 99/100] is of the opinion that 'The Duchess of Windsor's most lavish Cartier trinket was formed from another animal: a tiger lorgnette she had made in 1954, its rampant body and alert head forming the handle.'

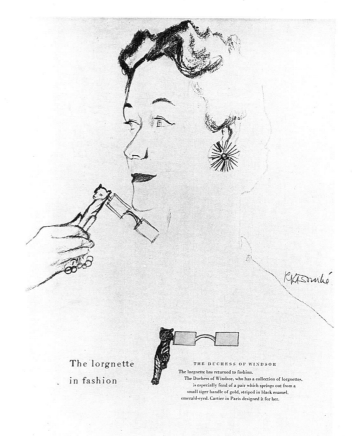

The lorgnette in fashion

THE DUCHESS OF WINDSOR

The lorgnette has returned to fashion.
The Duchess of Windsor, who has a collection of lorgnettes, is especially fond of a pair which springs out from a small tiger handle of gold, striped in black enamel, emerald-eyed. Cartier in Paris designed it for her.

below
189. AN 18 CARAT GOLD
AND ENAMEL HINGED BANGLE
French, probably circa 1960

The front designed as two confronted panther heads decorated with black enamel and with chains around their necks, grasping hoops between their jaws, two tapered hardwood sections forming the back, *maker's poinçon G. F., a stag's head between.*

A portrait by René Bouché
of the Duchess of Windsor with the tiger lorgnette (ill. 188), published in American Vogue in May, 1955.

Pearls

'I go down to Havant Castle every year to see her Grace's pearls, and I wipe every one of them myself, and let them lie on a sunny bank in the garden, in a westerly wind, for hours and days together. Their complexion would have been ruined had it not been for this treatment. Pearls are like girls, my Lord, they require quite as much attention.' ('Mr. Ruby', a character based upon the celebrated nineteenth-century Bond Street jeweller Charles Frederick Hancock in Benjamin Disreali's novel *Lothair*, published in 1870.)

This passage expresses the emotion which the pearl, that beautiful, naturally lustrous product, has aroused since times beyond memory. They are formed chiefly within the pearl oyster, the *Meleagrina margaritifera*, from a secreted substance called *conchidin* engulfing some foreign body, usually a shell-boring parasite.

Before the introduction of artificially cultured pearls early this century, the finest examples came from the Sooloo Archipelago on the north side of Borneo. They were also found off the coasts of Western Australia, a trade established by that once famous London jeweller E. W. Streeter, also in Sri Lanka, the Gulf of Panama and the Persian Gulf. According to Streeter, writing about a hundred years ago, pearl fishing in the latter area was not to be recommended because 'the natives along the coasts are so treacherous and fierce that . . . it is impossible for Europeans to work in safety.'

190. A SINGLE ROW PEARL NECKLACE
by Cartier, Paris

Strung with twenty-eight pearls graduating in size from 16.8 mm. to 9.2 mm. approximately, on an oval clasp of openwork design set with baguette, *calibré-* and circular-cut diamonds, *signed on the clasp: Cartier, Paris.*

The pearls weigh a total of 1261.33 grains; the weights of the five largest pearls are as follows: 120.09 grains; 76.39 grains; 68.96 grains; 67.89 grains; and 63.84 grains; *accompanied by a Gübelin report stating that the pearls are natural.*

191. A PEARL AND DIAMOND PENDANT
by Cartier, Paris, 1950

The large pearl of slightly baroque form, drilled and capped with diamonds, on a detachable stirrup-shaped diamond-set pendant fitting, *makers' poinçon; the pearl may be worn as a drop on the pearl necklace.* The pearl is stated to weigh 190.60 grains.

192. A PAIR OF PEARL AND DIAMOND EARCLIPS
by Van Cleef & Arpels, New York, 1957

One clip set with a black pearl measuring approximately 18.2 mm. within a border of pear-shaped and circular-cut diamonds, the other similarly set with a white pearl measuring approximately 18.1 mm., white gold mounts, *signed and numbered: Van Cleef & Arpels, N.Y., 28396.*

According to the archives of Van Cleef & Arpels, New York, these earclips, numbered 28396, were made in 1957 and purchased the following year.

opposite left
193. A CULTURED PEARL, EMERALD AND DIAMOND BRACELET
probably circa 1935

Designed as nine rows of cultured pearls, each row graduating from a larger centre, the two campana-shaped terminals *pavé-*set with circular-cut diamonds, the clasp of rosette design set with a cluster of emerald beads capped with small diamonds, and blue enamel beads encircled by rows of small diamonds.

opposite right
194. A PAIR OF 18 CARAT WHITE GOLD, CULTURED PEARL AND DIAMOND EARCLIPS
by Seaman Schepps

Each designed as a cluster of cultured pearls and claw-set brilliant-cut diamonds, *signed: Seaman Schepps.*

Seaman Schepps, who became one of New York's most famous jewellery designers, was born in that city in 1881. Spending some time in Paris, he opened his first shop in California before returning to New York where he settled in 1921. Schepps' work became especially popular during the 1930's and remained so for many years afterwards; in the 1960's his business was taken over by his daughter. A pioneer in the use of citrine quartz and cultured pearls, his jewels were at once colourful and sculptural. The use of polychrome stones mixed with rough and polished, but uncut, gems together with a variety of natural objects was particularly noteworthy.

above
195. A GOLD AND CULTURED PEARL CUFF BANGLE
probably by Belperron, circa 1940

The front designed as a large dart-shaped cluster of cultured pearls of various sizes drilled and set at random, *French gold poinçon.*

opposite, top to bottom left and right: ills. 196, 197, 198 and 199.

196. AN 18 CARAT GOLD, CULTURED PEARL AND DIAMOND CHOKER
by Darde & Fils, Paris, circa 1960

Designed as a rope of fifteen rows of cultured pearls on a tubular clasp, decorated with hexagonal motifs and set with brilliant-cut diamonds with a line of cultured pearls running across the centre.

197. A PAIR OF 18 CARAT GOLD, SEED PEARL AND DIAMOND EARRINGS
by Cartier, Paris

Each of turban design set with courses of seed pearls and capped by a single brilliant-cut diamond, *signed and numbered: Cartier, Paris, 01243.*

198 A PAIR OF GOLD, MABÉ PEARL AND DIAMOND EARCLIPS

Each with a single *mabé* pearl enclosed in a lattice *pavé*-set with brilliant-cut diamonds.

199. A PAIR OF CULTURED PEARL AND DIAMOND EARCLIPS
by Verdura, circa 1950

Each set with a *mabé* pearl within a gold border of twisted rope design set with circular-cut diamonds, *signed: Verdura.*

See note to ill. 171.

overleaf facing page: ills. 200 and 201.
200. A SINGLE ROW CULTURED PEARL NECKLACE
by Van Cleef & Arpels, 1964

Strung with twenty-nine cultured pearls graduating from approximately 15 mm. to 11 mm., on a barrel-shaped clasp *pavé*-set with baguette and brilliant-cut diamonds, *the clasp signed and numbered: VCA NY 34708.*

The Duke and Duchess of Windsor photographed in 1966 at the Marbeuf Cinema, Paris, where they attended a showing of The King's Story, *a film based upon the life of the Duke up to the end of his reign as Edward VIII. Note the pearl and diamond choker (ill. 196).*

According to the archives of Van Cleef & Arpels, New York, these pearls, numbered 34708, were strung especially for the Duchess of Windsor in 1964.

201. A PEARL AND DIAMOND RING
by Cartier, Paris, 1964

The pearl measuring approximately 18 mm. in diameter set within a gold and diamond border of *entrelac de rubans* on a reeded yellow gold shank, *signed and numbered: Cartier, Paris, P 9009.*

*T*he Duke and Duchess of
Windsor photographed by Maurice Tabard
in their Paris house in 1959. Note the bracelet of
crosses (ill. 92) and pearls including the necklace (ill.
200) and ring (ill. 201).

Diamonds

The diamond, which is composed of pure carbon, is the hardest and most brilliant of all the precious stones. It occurs in nature either colourless or variously tinted in shades ranging from pink, orange and yellow (ills. 202 and 203) to green, blue and black. For the most part they are found in India, Sumatra, Borneo, Brazil and South Africa, parts of North America, the Ural Mountains and Australia.

From India came the fabulous Koh-i-noor ('Mountain of Light') which, weighing 186 carats when presented by the East India Company in 1850 to the Duke of Windsor's great-grandmother, Queen Victoria, was then the largest diamond known. Its romantic history, quite as much as its tremendous size, enthralled visitors to the Great Exhibition of 1851, where it was shown when they read that it was supposed to have been worn by Karna, King of Anga, slain in battle some three-thousand years before the birth of Christ! In 1852 *Punch* published the cartoon 'The Poor Old Koh-i-noor Again!' referring to the stone's re-cutting with the assistance of the Duke of Wellington at R. & S. Garrard & Co.'s premises by Voorzanger and Fedder, two representatives of M.E. Coster's diamond-cutting workshops in Amsterdam.

Queen Mary, the Duke of Windsor's mother, was also the recipient of important diamonds, notably the six large brilliants and ninety-six smaller stones given her in 1910 by the Union of South Africa. These had been cleaved from the literally gigantic Cullinan diamond, a colossus of 3,025 carats part of which, now called the Star of Africa, joined the Crown Jewels. Discovered in the workings of a South African mine in 1905, it originally had been presented to Edward VII by the people of the Transvaal. Owing to its weight, flawless character and enormous value, the cutting of the stone presented a unique challenge to Asscher's of Amsterdam, who had been entrusted with the operation; their proprietor fainted under the emotional strain.

part-title page, top to bottom: ills. 202 and 203.

202. A PAIR OF FANCY YELLOW DIAMOND EARCLIPS
mounted by Cartier, Paris, 1968

Each with a larger pear-shaped and a circular-cut diamond, the mounts *pavé*-set with brilliant-cut stones, *signed: Monture Cartier and numbered: 2860*. The following weights are recorded in Cartier's archives: two pear-shaped diamonds: 8.13 and 8.01 carats; two brilliant-cut diamonds: 5.17 and 5.18 carats; two hundred and fifty-two brilliant-cut diamonds: 15.56 carats.

203. A PAIR OF YELLOW DIAMOND LAPEL CLIPS
by Harry Winston, 1948

Each with a pear-shaped stone weighing 40.81 and 52.13 carats respectively, claw-set within a border of gold corded wire scroll motifs, set at intervals with brilliant-cut diamonds.

'I am enclosing several designs for the two canary diamonds which I hope will please you,' wrote Harry Winston to the Duchess of Windsor on 29th January, 1948. His letter continued, '. . . The two stones weigh approximately 92.95 carats and are priceless! Never before in my experience have I seen a pair of pear-shaped canary diamonds so wonderfully matched—both because of their exquisite brilliancy and lustre and their unusually large size. It is due only to existing conditions in the world today that we were able to purchase diamonds such as these from old estates of royalty. In fact, they are so magnificent, that were it not you I am offering them to—I should keep them here as showpieces with my other jewels.' Winston then informed the Duchess that he had set the diamonds, 'in a very charming gold setting so that you can wear them now. When you return they can be reset in your chosen design.' Finishing his letter, Winston thought that he would be leaving New York the following week. 'If this is the case,' he wrote, 'I will telephone you and discuss the matter with you. I trust you like them as well as we do. I do hope that you are enjoying your holiday and are having pleasant weather. The unusually cold weather in New York makes my thoughts roam southward.'

In her reply of 2nd February, 1948, the Duchess told Harry Winston that, 'The canary diamonds are certainly very interesting and in my opinion the present setting could not be improved upon . . . If we can find a way to acquire these stones I would of course have to have two medium size yellow diamond earrings [to match] . . . I can't think of anything I would rather have than these two diamonds. I have worn them twice and they have caused a sensation—only one person asking what they were. Mr Boettches suspected you at once! If you have anything that might do as earrings would you send them down as I have nothing suitable . . . '

opposite, top to bottom: ills. 204, 205, 206 and 207.

204. A PLATINUM AND DIAMOND NECKLACE
by Cartier, Paris

In the form of a *rivière* of brilliant-cut diamonds *pavé*-set in square bezels slightly graduated in size from the front, the clasp set with three baguette diamonds, *the gold tongue piece signed: Cartier, Paris.*

The Duchess of Windsor often wore this necklace with the large sapphire pendant (ill. 119).

205. A CULTURED PEARL AND DIAMOND BAR BROOCH/PENDANT HANGER
by Darde & Fils, Paris, circa 1960

Designed as an arched row of brillant- and eight-cut diamonds with a cultured pearl, drilled and set with a small diamond, at each terminal, the centre encircled by a detachable pendant loop *pavé*-set with brilliant-cut diamonds.

Darde & Fils, of 12, rue St. Gilles, Paris 3ᵉ, were working jewellers well known in the Parisian trade for the fine quality of their productions. Their poinçon, DF, a *fleur-de-lys* between, was registered on 28th December, 1955, and withdrawn on 27th January, 1970, at about the time of the firm's closure.

206. A DIAMOND CLIP LORGNETTE
by Van Cleef & Arpels, New York, circa 1935

Of stylized stirrup-shaped design, *pavé*-set throughout with baguette and circular-cut stones, *signed and numbered: Van Cleef & Arpels N.Y., number illegible.*

207. A DIAMOND DRESS SUITE
by Cartier, London, 1935

Comprising: a pair of cufflinks, each circular link *pavé*-set with brilliant-cut diamonds, one with the letter W set with baguette diamonds, the other with the letter E similarly set, one bar fitting *inscribed and dated: Wallis 19.6.35,* the other *inscribed and dated: David 23.6.35,* both *signed: Cartier, London;* three Buttons, all with the letter E, two of the fittings *inscribed respectively: Hold Tight* and: *E 7/5/35;* and a Stud with the intial E.

The 19th June, 1935, was Mrs Simpson's 39th birthday. The Jubilee celebrations of King George V and Queen Mary on 6th May, 1935, were followed the next evening by a reception given by Edward, Prince of Wales at Buckingham Palace. The cryptic inscription *E 7/5/35* would therefore appear to refer to this event.

'Hold tight' and similar phrases were often employed by the Duke and Duchess of Windsor in their correspondence before their marriage. See, for instance, his 'Hold me tight please' and 'a boy loves a girl more and more and is holding her so tight these trying days of waiting' in letters of 14th and 24th October, 1936, and her 'I'm holding you tighter than ever' in one of 6th December, 1936. Quoted on pp. 225/7 and 243 of *Wallis and Edward, Letters 1931-1937: the Intimate Correspondence of the Duke and Duchess of Windsor,* edited by Michael Bloch, published in the UK by Weidenfeld and Nicolson (hardback) and Penguin Books (paperback), and in the USA by Summit Books Inc.; hereinafter referred to as *Letters.* See ill. 137.

The 23rd June, 1935, was Edward, Prince of Wales' 41st birthday. See ills. 92 (8) and 93 (1).

opposite, top to bottom: ills. 208 and 209.

208. A DIAMOND CROSSOVER BANGLE
by Cartier, Paris, 1956

The front set with six larger step-cut stones within a border of circular-cut diamonds, the back designed as a line of *carré* diamonds between courses of circular-cut stones, mounted in platinum, *makers' poinçon.* The following weights are recorded in Cartier's archives: the six principal step-cut diamonds weigh a total of 26.55 carats; thirty *carré* diamonds: 16.03 carats; twelve baguette diamonds: 3.58 carats; two hundred and forty-three brilliant-cut diamonds: 7.88 carats.

209. A PAIR OF DIAMOND EARCLIPS
by Cartier, Paris, 1962

Each designed as an informal cluster of pear-shaped diamonds, *inscribed: R 2319; makers' poinçon for Cartier.* The weights of the largest pear-shaped diamonds are as follows: 4.48; 3.54; 2.04 carats; 5.06; 3.89; 1.85 carats.

below
210. A GOLD AND DIAMOND ETERNITY RING
by Darde & Fils, Paris, circa 1962

Designed as a single row of baguette diamonds between borders of gold bands.

opposite, top to bottom: ills. 213. and 211,

211. AN 18 CARAT GOLD AND DIAMOND DRESS RING
French, circa 1950

The wide tonneau-shaped bezel *pavé*-set with four rows of cushion-shaped diamonds in a honeycomb design.

below right:
212. A PAIR OF 18 CARAT GOLD AND DIAMOND EARCLIPS
French, circa 1945

Each designed as a scrolled wing motif, *pavé*-set with cushion-shaped and brilliant- and eight-cut diamonds.

213. A DIAMOND BROOCH
by Harry Winston, New York, 1956

Designed as a flowerhead, the larger step-cut stone mounted at the centre within a border of nine pear-shaped stones.

below left
214. A DIAMOND RING
by Harry Winston, 1950

The cushion-shaped stone weighing 31.26 carats, claw-set between tapered baguette diamond single stone shoulders; *accompanied by a report from the Gemological Institute of America* stating that the stone is 'D' colour with a clarity of VS 2, together with the original worksheet stating that the clarity of this stone is improvable; *accompanied by a Gübelin report stating that this stone is a type II A diamond, and commenting that diamonds showing a high degree of brilliancy like the specimen are sometimes broadly called Golconda in trade circles, in recollection of the aspect of ancient fine diamonds.*

Originally owned by Evalyn Walsh McLean, the famous Washington hostess, the '31 carat McLean diamond' seen here is mentioned by Laurence S. Krashes in his book, *Harry Winston—The Ultimate Jeweler.* Mrs McLean, whose passion for fine jewels was well known, stated in her autobiography, '. . . when I neglect to wear jewels, astute members of my family call in doctors because it is a sign I'm becoming ill.'

Mrs McLean is probably best remembered as an owner of the celebrated Hope diamond, which she purchased from Pierre Cartier in 1911. Three years earlier, while honeymooning in Paris, she bought the 94.80 carat pear-shaped diamond called the 'Star of the East', which she frequently wore beneath the Hope diamond on a necklace. In 1949, two years after her death, Harry Winston purchased Mrs McLean's collection of jewelry, which included all three above-mentioned diamonds in addition to other fine stones. The 'McLean' diamond was sold in May the following year to the Duke and Duchess of Windsor.

Photos Credits

Michael Bloch. 39 right, 42 right, 44, 49, 52 bottom right, 52 top, 66, 70 left, 71, 73, 74. BBC. 58 left. Bettmann Archive. 33 top, 36, 62, 72 bottom. Camera Press. 30 left, 33 bottom, 45, 55 right, 58, 78, 79. Illustrated London News. Kenro Izu. 120, 121, 150, 151, 201, 77. Lady Alexandra Metcalfe. 34 bottom right. National Portrait Gallery, London. 23 top, 24, 27 left, 39 left. Photo Source. 23 center right, 27 right, 32 right, 48 left, 51, 53 left, 54 left, 61 bottom, 64, 70 left. Popperphoto. 23 center left and bottom, 26, 27 left, 28, 31, 32 left, 34 top, 35, 37, 42 left, 47, 48 left, 52 bottom left, 57, 61 top right, 64 left, 76, 78. Royal Archives, Windsor Castle. 20. Sothebys. 6-16, 30 right, 34 bottom left, 38, 46 left, 56, 59 right, 61 top left, 63, 65 right, 67 left, 68, 69. Sunday Times. 77.